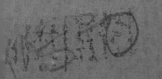

ONE MAN, ONE VOTE

THE HISTORY OF THE AFRICAN-AMERICAN VOTE IN THE UNITED STATES

The League of Women Voters of Cleveland Educational Fund
in cooperation with Cleveland State University

ACKNOWLEDGMENTS

The League of Women Voters of Cleveland Educational Fund (LWVCEF) appreciates the generous support of the following sponsors and special contributors which made possible the publication of *One Man, One Vote: The History of the African-American Vote in the United States.*

Primary Sponsors
The George Gund Foundation
The Cleveland Foundation
Cleveland State University

Sponsors
Emerson Press Inc.
TRW, Inc.
United Black Fund of Greater Cleveland, Inc.

The LWVCEF would like to thank Cleveland State University President John A. Flower, Vice President for University Relations and Development August Napoli, and Chair of the Department of History Thomas Campbell, who gave their valuable support and assistance to the publication of *One Man, One Vote* in conjunction with the university's 25th anniversary.

A special thank you to Nancy Stella of the Joint Center for Political and Economic Studies in Washington, D.C. which provided the valuable information on black elected officials included as addenda to this book. The LWVCEF also wishes to thank the Cleveland Alliance of Black School Educators for their encouragement and support of this project.

Special Credit:
Patricia Sweet, project manager, LWVCEF
Carolyn Jefferson, principal author, LWVCEF
Cassandra Talerico, assistant writer and researcher, LWVCEF
Dennis Dooley, editorial consultant
Margaret Rosenfield, project consultant
Jean Robejsek, technical coordinator, LWVCEF
Jo-Ann Dontenville, layout and design, Cleveland State University

City of Cleveland

MICHAEL R. WHITE, MAYOR

DEDICATION BY

DEDICATION BY

Michael R. White
Mayor, City of Cleveland

As a mayor of a major American city and an African-American, I applaud the efforts and research of the League of Women Voters of Cleveland Educational Fund and Carolyn Jefferson, the principal author, for undertaking the task of compiling "One Man, One Vote: The History of the African-American Vote in the United States." It is an important and historic document.

This book should be required reading for every school child in America, as well as for all those interested and involved in the electoral process. It is not only the story of a people and their right to vote, but it is also the story of America: how this country has struggled to overcome the injustices and obstacles faced by a segment of its people.

I am honored that the League has chosen to release this book in Cleveland during the 17th Annual Convention of the National Conference of Black Mayors. Many of those attending the convention have benefited from the sacrifices documented in the following pages.

I hope that this literary achievement will serve as a catalyst for more concentrated research and become a major point of reference for those who desire to learn of our struggle.

TABLE OF CONTENTS

PREFACE

One Man, One Vote: The History of the African-American Vote in the United States tells the story of that historic struggle and explores the contributions African-Americans have made to the democratic process. The intent of this history is to reinforce our knowledge of, and pride in, these accomplishments and to encourage full participation in American government among voting groups whose participation has traditionally been low.

The determination of African-Americans to gain full citizenship and the right to vote (sometimes called the franchise or enfranchisement) was fueled by the realization that African-Americans are an important segment of the American population, that they have a stake in the "system," and that their political participation can make a difference. If African-Americans are to make further gains and continue to be heard in government, participation in the voting process must continue to grow.

One Man, One Vote looks at the role American legal principles have played in determining the extent to which African-Americans have participated in the political process.

Several areas of interest are covered, including the contributions of African-American leaders and organizations to the electoral system; legislation that has been key to African-American enfranchisement; organizations that have fostered African-American voter participation; and landmark Supreme Court cases related to voter registration and participation. Selected statistical information on African-American elected officials and voters, both past and present, has also been included.

A bibliography and resources are provided for further study.

As Supreme Court Justice Thurgood Marshall has eloquently written on the subject of U.S. legislative history and African-Americans:

> *What is striking is the role legal principles have played throughout America's history in determining the condition of Negroes. They were enslaved by law, emancipated by law, disenfranchised and segregated by law; and finally, they have begun to win equality by law. Along the way, new constitutional principles have emerged to meet the challenges of a changing society. The progress has been dramatic, and it will continue.* [1]

Marching for full voting rights.

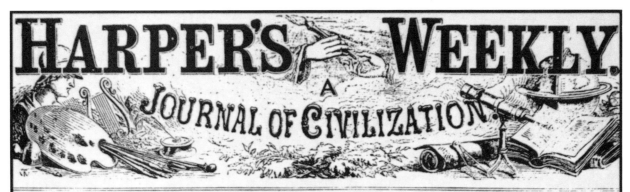

HARPER'S WEEKLY.

A JOURNAL OF CIVILIZATION.

VOL. XI.—No. 568.]   NEW YORK, SATURDAY, NOVEMBER 16, 1867.   [SINGLE COPIES TEN CENTS. $4.00 PER YEAR IN ADVANCE.

Entered according to Act of Congress, in the Year 1867, by Harper & Brothers, in the Clerk's Office of the District Court for the Southern District of New York.

"Harper's Weekly"
November, 16, 1867

"Last Sunday [we] started on a mighty walk . . . . They told us we wouldn't get here."

▶ *... It was declared by all reputable authorities*
▶ *that the fate of the Negro race in the United States*
▶ *was extinction and death, and that what tuberculosis*
▶ *did not do, crime and inefficiency would finish. And,*
▶ *finally, it was said by the Negroes themselves, almost*
▶ *unanimously, that real effective organization for the*
▶ *attainment of the rights of black men in America was*
▶ *impossible.*
▶   *But we disregarded the advice of our friends.*
▶ *We went in for agitation. We pushed our way into*
▶ *the courts. We demanded the right to vote. We*
▶ *urged and pushed our children into college.... We*
▶ *stand today at the threshold of a new*
▶ *generation...with the reappearance of the black man*
▶ *in Congress and, what is more important, with the*
▶ *emergence of an independent Negro vote....* [2]
▶
▶ Dr. W.E.B. DuBois's Keynote address, 20th
▶ Anniversary NAACP Conference, June 27, 1929.
▶

The first hurdle the march toward African-American suffrage had to overcome was, ironically, the fundamental law of the United States—the U.S. Constitution.

As the American experiment passed its first half-century in 1839 and moved into the 1850s, the only people permitted to vote in most states were free, white, male property owners over twenty-one years of age. Indeed, this had been the intent of the Constitution's framers. Furthermore, individual states were allowed to impose qualifications in addition to those established in the U.S. Constitution.

The constitutional right to vote did not extend to slaves or indentured servants. Since slaves were considered to be property, not citizens, it was argued that they had no right to vote. Most African-Americans were slaves during this time, and hence could not be property owners themselves, leaving them doubly unqualified, in the eyes of the law, to participate in electoral politics. The United States Supreme Court affirmed this position in the *Dred Scott v. Sanford* decision of 1857, with Chief Justice Roger B. Taney stating that African-Americans, whether slaves or free, did not have and had never had any legal standing in the courts of the United States.[3] Free African-Americans thus fared no better than slaves in their early attempts at political participation.

But a door had been left open by the framers.

Although the Constitution did not directly guarantee voting rights for everyone, it did provide the means for individual states to extend this right to those who were disenfranchised. The Civil War and the events that followed during the Reconstruction period (1865-1877) led to unprecedented social and political changes that began slowly to build momentum. It would take 100 years, but the long battle to secure voting rights begun by African-Americans at the end of the Civil War in 1865 would eventually culminate in the passage of the Voting Rights Act of 1965.

During Reconstruction, the Thirteenth, Fourteenth, and Fifteenth Amendments to the Constitution were passed. These Amendments, respectively, abolished slavery, granted citizenship, and granted the right to vote to African-American men. (African-American women would have to wait until 1920.) However, the Amendments failed to provide the guarantees their framers had envisioned. The scope of these provisions was challenged repeatedly in the courts and, in a series of U.S. Supreme Court decisions handed down between 1876 and 1906, African-Americans were effectively stripped of the rights that the Reconstruction Amendments had been intended to guarantee.

The Reconstruction era saw the election of African-Americans to numerous political offices despite the challenges being brought even then against the Reconstruction Amendments. Since African-Americans outnumbered whites in several southern states, once they were able to exercise their voting rights, they often elected African-Americans to official positions. Many white Southerners viewed the increasing number of African-American office holders as a threat to their traditional way of life. This eventually led to the creation of measures designed to restrict the political power of the newly enfranchised African-Americans.[4]

In some areas, mobs used threats and intimidation to keep African-American voters away from the polls. A Congressional committee reported in 1892 that in some southern states white mobs threatened African-Americans with a return to slavery unless they swore to vote for the mob's candidate. Historically, "Black Codes" written into many southern state constitutions, poll taxes, and literacy tests were among the other tactics used to discourage or prohibit African-Americans from voting. These measures, coupled with the changing interpretations of the Reconstruction Amendments, gave rise to state legislation that greatly diminished the number of African-American voters. In 1896, for example, 130,334 African-Americans were registered to vote in Louisiana. By 1900 the number had dropped to 5,320. [5]

It was not until 1964 that the poll tax, which effectively denied poor people their right as citizens to vote, would finally be abolished with the passage of the Twenty-fourth Amendment. Even after the passage of the Civil Rights Act of 1964 and Voting Rights Act of 1965, many African-Americans still experienced resistance when exercising their right to vote in certain parts of the United States.

The road to black suffrage was long and hard-fought. One hundred years of detours and road blocks often impeded progress. Yet, progress was made, thanks largely to determined African-Americans who knew that they could only obtain political power through participation in government. Indeed, the dramatic strides made by a people once themselves considered property only underscores the political power of the African-American vote.

Peachtree, Ala.: Negroes—the newest power in deep south politics—flock to this polling place in a store called, "The Sugar Shack," in rural Blackbelt, Ala., as they vote in large numbers for the first time in history. The major issue in the Democratic primary was segregation. 5/5/66

1

A MIGHTY WALK: THE 100-YEAR-LONG MARCH TO THE BALLOT BOX

African-Americans will forever hold a unique place in the history of the United States as the only group of individuals to have been legally enslaved. Their history does not parallel that of other Americans--a history that is identified with freedom, independence, equality, and political power.

▸ *The impact of black slavery on American colonial life*
▸ *was pervasive, but as a factor in politics, the slave was*
▸ *usually outside specific political discussion. The role of*
▸ *the slave was assumed and unstated. The slaves, who*
▸ *of course had no political spokesman, were barred from*
▸ *the traditional American expectations of a better life, of*
▸ *progress, of working to improve one's status, with the*
▸ *result that the slave was alienated from the main-*
▸ *stream of American life.* [1]

This alienation lay behind many of the problems that both African-Americans and whites would face after the Civil War. The Reconstruction Period (1865-1877) was to have a profound effect on African-Americans and the role they in turn would play in shaping the history of the United States, for Reconstruction would lay the groundwork for the social, economic, and political changes that completed the first leg of the road to African-American suffrage.

THE RECONSTRUCTION AMENDMENTS

Reconstruction, an attempt to smoothly reunite the North and South, developed around four plans: Lincoln's Plan (1865); Johnson's Plan (1865-1866); Congress's Plan (1866-1867); Congress's Second Plan (1867-1877).[2] This era also saw the passage of three Amendments to the United States Constitution: Amendments 13, 14, and 15, often referred to as the **Reconstruction Amendments.** These amendments individually addressed specific issues germane to ensuring the rights and privileges of citizenship for African-Americans. Collectively, these amendments represented unprecedented change in the social, economic, and political status quo.

"And there were those who said that we could get there only over their dead bodies, but all the world today knows that we are here and that we are standing before the forces of power ... 'We ain't goin' let nobody turn us around.'"

Bettmann Archive

Protecting Negroes from White Blacklash Woodcut 1868.

5

Thirteenth Amendment (1865)

Section 1. Neither slavery nor involuntary servitude, except as a punishment for crime whereof the party shall have been duly convicted, shall exist within the United States, or any place subject to their jurisdiction.

Fourteenth Amendment (1868)

Section 1. All persons born or naturalized in the United States, and subject to the jurisdiction thereof, are citizens of the United States and of the state wherein they reside. No state shall make or enforce any law which shall abridge the privileges or immunities of citizens of the United States; nor shall any state deprive any person of life, liberty, or property without due process of law; nor deny to any person within its jurisdiction the equal protection of the law.

Section 2. Representatives shall be apportioned among the several States according to their respective numbers, counting the whole number of persons in each state, excluding Indians not taxed. But when the right to vote at any election for the choice of electors for president and vice-president of the United States, representatives in Congress, the executive and judicial officers of a State, or the members of the legislature thereof, is denied to any of the male inhabitants of such state being of twenty-one years of age, and citizens of the United States, or in any way abridged, except for participation in rebellion or other crime, the basis of representation therein shall be reduced in the proportion which the number of such male citizens shall bear to the whole number of male citizens twenty-one years of age in such state.

Section 3. No person shall be a Senator or Representative in Congress, or elector of President and Vice President, or hold any office, civil or military, under the United States, or under any state, who, having previously taken an oath, as a member of Congress, or as an officer of the United States, or as a member of any state legislature, or as an executive or judicial officer of any state shall have engaged in insurrection or rebellion against the same, or given aid or comfort to the enemies thereof. But Congress may, by a vote of two-thirds of each house, remove such disability.

Section 4. The validity of the public debt of the United States, authorized by law, including debts incurred for payment of pensions and bounties for services in suppressing insurrection or rebellion, shall not be questioned. But neither the United States nor any state shall assume or pay any debt or obligation incurred in aid of insurrection or rebellion against the United States, or any claim for the loss or emancipation of any slave; but all such debts, obligations, and claims shall be held illegal and void.

Fifteenth Amendment (1890)

Section 1. The right of citizens of the United States to vote shall not be denied or abridged by the United States or by any State, on account of race, color, or previous condition of servitude.

THE BLACK CODES

The Thirteenth Amendment, proposed on January 31, 1865 and ratified on December 18, 1865, legally abolished slavery in the United States. Lincoln's Emancipation Proclamation had only abolished slavery in those states that were warring against the Union. As a result, the southern U.S. border states still legally maintained slavery until the Thirteenth Amendment was ratified. But counter tactics by those who would deny African-Americans the full exercise of their newly affirmed rights were already underway.

In the same year the Thirteenth Amendment was passed, the first **"Black Codes"** were passed by southern legislatures. Black Codes were laws similar to the Slave Codes, being designed with the intention of drastically limiting the rights of the newly freed slaves. The Civil War eliminated the South's source of free labor. The implementation of the Black Codes was one of the South's attempts to maintain a source of cheap plantation labor while giving African-Americans a new legal status. Consequently many of the Codes outlined labor and vagrancy statutes that were written to keep African-Americans in a state of peonage and to provide them with legal status little better than that which they had as slaves.[3]

In addition to highly restrictive labor statutes, the Black Codes prohibited interracial marriages, although they did recognize marriage between African-Americans as being legal. African-Americans were allowed to testify in court, but in some states the Black Codes only permitted blacks to testify against other blacks; and the Codes restricted African-Americans in the rental, purchase and ownership of property. The Black Codes varied in their provisions but generally they severely limited African-Americans' employment and economic opportunities, denied them the right to vote, kept them off juries, and ensured segregated public facilities.

President Andrew Johnson's restoration of home rule to the southern states, coupled with lack of adequate numbers of African-American state representatives to vote against the Black Codes, facilitated their passage. The following excerpts from the Mississippi Constitution reveal the extent to which the state legislatures were prepared to go to maintain the pre-war status quo.

Section 1. Be it enacted by the legislature of the state of Mississippi, that all rogues and vagabonds, idle and dissipated persons, beggars, jugglers, or persons practising unlawful games or plays, run-aways, common drunkards, common nightwalkers, pilferers, lewd, wanton, or lascivious persons, in speech or behavior, common railers and brawlers, persons who neglect their calling or employment, misspend what they earn, or do not provide for the support of themselves or their families or dependents, and all other idle and disorderly persons, including all who neglect all lawful business, or habitually misspend their time by frequenting houses of ill-fame, gaming houses, or tippling shops, shall be deemed and considered vagrants under the provisions of this act; and, on conviction thereof, shall be fined not exceeding $100, with all accruing costs, and be imprisoned at the discretion of the court not exceeding ten days.

Section 2. Be it further enacted, that all freedmen, free Negroes, and mulattoes in this state over the age of eighteen years found on the second Monday in January 1866, or thereafter, with no lawful employment or business, or found unlawfully assembling themselves together either in the day or nighttime, and all white persons so assembling with freedmen, free Negroes, or mulattoes, or usually associating with freedmen, free Negroes, or mulattoes on terms of equality, or living in adultery or fornication with a freedwoman, free Negro, or mulatto, shall be deemed vagrants; and, on conviction thereof, shall be fined in the sum of not exceeding, in the case of a freedman, free Negro, or mulatto, $50, and a white man, $200, and imprisoned at the discretion of the court, the free Negro not exceeding ten days, and the white man not exceeding six months....

Section 5. Be it further enacted, that all fines and forfeitures collected under the provisions of this act shall be paid into the county treasury for general county purposes; and in case any freedman, free Negro, or mulatto shall fail for five days after the imposition of any fine or forfeiture upon him or her for violation of any of the provisions of this act to pay the same, that it shall be, and is hereby made, the duty of the sheriff of the proper county to hire out said freedman, free Negro, or mulatto to any person who will, for the shortest period of service, pay said fine or forfeiture and all costs: Provided, a preference shall be given to the employer, if there be one, in which case the employer, shall be entitled to deduct and retain the amount so paid from the wages of such freedman, free Negro, or mulatto then due or to become due; and in case such freedman, free Negro, or mulatto cannot be hired out, he or she may be dealt with as a pauper....

Section 7. Be it further enacted, that if any

- freedman, free Negro, or mulatto shall fail or
- refuse to pay any tax levied acording to the
- provisions of the 6th Section of this act, it shall
- be prima facie evidence of vagrancy, and it shall
- be the duty of the sheriff to arrest such freed-
- man, free Negro, or mulatto, or such persons
- refusing or neglecting to pay such tax, and
- proceed at once to hire, for the shortest time,
- such delinquent taxpayer to anyone who will
- pay the said tax, with accruing costs, giving
- preference to the employer, if there be one.
- **Section 8.** Be it further enacted, that any person
- feeling himself or herself aggrieved by the
- judgment of any justice of the peace, mayor or
- alderman in cases arising under this act may,
- within five days, appeal to the next term of the
- county court of the proper county, upon giving
- bond and security in a sum not less that $25 nor
- more than $150, conditioned to appear and
- prosecute said appeal, and abide by the judg-
- ment of the county court, and said appeal shall
- be tried de novo in the county court, and the
- decision of said court shall be final. [4]

The newly freed slaves were for the most part without formal education, employment, and permanent residences. By taking advantage of these conditions to classify African-Americans as vagrants, beggars, or criminals, the white legislatures of Mississippi and other states systematically deprived much of their African-American population of the rights and privileges accorded to all other citizens of the state.

Large numbers of African-Americans became the victims of murders, lynchings, and vicious attacks on property they owned. The Ku Klux Klan was formed in 1866 in Tennessee, initially as a social club.[5] Through intimidation, violence, and death, this vigilante organization undertook to enforce the traditional southern view regarding the status of African-Americans.

"JIM CROW LAWS"

Many of the Black Codes were dismantled by Radical Reconstruction in 1867. However similar restrictions resurfaced in the 1890's by the enactment of **"Jim Crow"** laws. Jim Crow laws were a system of customs and laws in the southern states designed to segregate African-Americans from white society (see box). Gradually, the words "Jim Crow" would be applied to the legal segregation of African-Americans and whites in everyday life, including segregation in schools, transportation systems, theaters, parks, and drinking fountains. In Oklahoma, for example, Jim Crow laws passed in the twentieth century demanded whites and African-Americans use separate telephone booths. In Arkansas gambling halls, African-Americans and whites had to play at separate tables. Some southern courts even resorted to using separate Bibles for swearing in witnesses.

The phrase "Jim Crow" dates from 1830. Walking out of his Baltimore theater, Thomas Rice, a famous white entertainer, saw a Negro singer-dancer performing in the alley. Rice "borrowed" the man's dance routine and costume and enlarged on the song he was singing. Rice made the words famous: "Wheel about, turn about, dance just so— everytime I wheel about I shout Jim Crow." While whites found Rice's character funny and cute, Negroes found it hateful. Like another white invention, "Uncle Tom," which Negroes used to describe a man afraid to stand up for his rights, Negroes used "Jim Crow" to refer to the many kinds of discrimination they faced. [6]

THE FREEDMEN'S BUREAU

After the Thirteenth Amendment took effect, four million slaves left the plantations. These **freedmen,** as they were called, now were thrust into the same mainstream society that had alienated them. They had no land of their own, no education, and for the most part, no destination. Having been systematically deprived of education and opportunity, they were without the means to participate in or contribute to southern society.

Initially, assistance for the freedmen was forthcoming from both private sources and the U.S. government. In the North, civic and religious groups formed relief associations that shipped food, clothing, and crop seeds to the South. But, although numerous private freedmen's relief societies existed, the intervention of the federal government was also needed. At the insistence of General Sherman and other union generals, and in response to the North's demand that the federal government step in to protect the former slaves, Congress in March 1865 set up the Bureau of Refugees, Freedmen, and Abandoned Lands. This agency, established as part of the War Department, was popularly known as the **Freedmen's Bureau**.

Originally established for a one-year period, the Bureau's life was later extended until 1869. During the five years of its existence, the Freedmen's Bureau provided many services needed by the newly freed slaves. It set up courts, provided medical care and hospitals, fed the hungry, and negotiated to ensure a fair wage for laborers once they found employment. It also allotted small tracts of land and later leased and sold land to the freedmen, but this policy had to be canceled when President Andrew Johnson, seeking to fulfill Lincoln's Reconstruction Plan, issued pardons to former Confederates, which entitled the pardoned rebels to reclaim their previously confiscated land.

The Bureau's greatest success was in education. It established schools and provided textbooks for them. Among the more than 3,000 schools established was Howard University, named for the Bureau's first administrator, General Oliver Howard. In some cases poor whites were able to take advantage of the Freedmen's Bureau programs.

The Bureau, however, often came under attack by both the South and North. As part of the War Department, the Freedmen's Bureau was under military authority, and its officials were given almost complete control over the affairs of African-Americans. Many of the Bureau's officials became powerful forces in southern state governments and used their power for selfish gain. This abuse of power led to widespread distrust of the entire Bureau in the South.

While southern whites felt additional antipathy toward the Bureau because it was working to educate African-Americans and to secure equal treatment by employers of their employees, many Northerners viewed the Bureau as an expensive agency that could not be justified in peace time. Many whites believed the federal government was interfering in local affairs and that the Freedmen's Bureau had its own agenda: establishing a strong Republican Party in the South by enfranchising African-Americans. At one point, Congress had to override a Presidential veto in order to extend the life of the Bureau.

RADICAL RECONSTRUCTION

When Congress met in December 1865, radicals led by Thaddeus Stevens in the U.S. House of Representatives and Charles Sumner in the U.S. Senate proposed a series of bills designed to strengthen the Freedmen's Bureau and protect the rights of the African-American freedmen. Spurred by the efforts of these two men and by the southern states rapid establishment of the Black Codes, Congress voted to override the veto of President Andrew Johnson and passed the Reconstruction Act of 1867.

This act subdivided the South, excluding Tennessee, into five military districts. Each was under a commander who had the authority to remove civilians from public office, regulate voter registration, and act to ensure equal rights for African-Americans. The state governments that had existed under the Confederacy were declared illegal, and the rights of ex-confederate leaders were suspended. Specific steps by which new state governments could be formed, including constitutional conventions, were defined.

The Reconstruction Act ushered in what would become known as **Radical Reconstruction**. It was intended to inaugurate a new social order throughout the South. No southern state could be readmitted to the Union until it had ratified the Fourteenth Amendment. The **Fourteenth Amendment** to the U.S. Constitution, proposed on June 13, 1866, and ratified on July 28, 1868, proclaimed citizenship for African-Americans. As full citizens, African-Americans could no longer be deprived of the rights accorded other citizens. In addition, each state's constitution had to meet the approval of both the voters in that state and the United States Congress. (Tennessee, which had approved the Fourteenth Amendment in 1866, was exempt from this process.) [7]

In order to develop new state constitutions, constitutional conventions were called in the southern states. These assemblies wrote and adopted constitutions that set forth new guidelines for the state governments. African-Americans took part in the conventions; they were particularly active in South Carolina where they made up a majority of the delegates and in Louisiana where they were equal in number to white delegates.

The new state constitutions brought badly needed reforms. Nearly all extended property rights to women, set up the first statewide systems of education, placed the judiciary under popular control, created new tax systems with more nearly uniform assessment methods, and established welfare agencies such as orphanages, institutions for the mentally ill, and schools for the blind and the deaf. In addition, the constitutions abolished ownership of property as a qualification for voting and holding office.

The conventions worked to write laws that would serve all the citizens and yet not be so offensive to conservative whites that they would be rejected at the polls. The state constitutions framed at this time remained in effect for many years.

The **Fifteenth Amendment**, the last of the Reconstruction Amendments, was proposed February 26, 1869, and ratified March 30, 1870. It declared the right of African-American men to vote. However, it allowed the individual states to establish their own requirements and qualifications for voting. African-Americans were soon participating actively in the elections in the South, but that participation was to be short-lived.

Amendments Thirteen, Fourteen, and Fifteen were accepted reluctantly by southern whites and challenged repeatedly. As we have seen, they turned out to be something less than the effective guarantees they were meant to be. Emancipation had altered the form but not the substance of African-Americans' political status.

THREATS AND INTIMIDATION

During 1865 and 1866, before most southern states had adopted their new constitutions, African-Americans in a number of southern cities held conventions to discuss the problems they faced in exercising their rights of citizenship. They appealed to the nation for support and protection, the support and protection guaranteed by the U.S. Constitution to all citizens of the United States. The following excerpt from a speech made at a convention in Alexandria, Virginia, in August 1865 reflects their perception of their problem and their solution for gaining full citizenship rights.

▶ *AN ADDRESS TO THE LOYAL CITIZENS AND*
▶ *CONGRESS OF THE UNITED STATES OF*
▶ *AMERICA, AUGUST 1865*
▶ We the undersigned members of a Convention
▶ of colored citizens of the State of Virginia, would
▶ respectfully represent that, although we have

been held slaves, and denied recognition as a
constituent of your nationality for almost the
entire period of the duration of your government, and that by your *permission* we have been
denied either home or country, and deprived of
the dearest rights of human nature: yet when
you and our immediate oppressors met in
deadly conflict upon the field of battle.... *we*,
with scarce an exception, in our inmost souls
espoused your cause, and watched, and prayed,
and wanted and labored for your success. ...
Well, the war is over, the rebellion is "put
down", and we are declared free. ... In one
word, the only salvation for us besides the
power of the Government, is in the *possession of
the ballot*. Give us this, and we will protect
ourselves. ... All we ask is an equal chance with
the white traitors varnished and japanned with
the oath of amnesty. Can you deny us this and
still keep faith with us?[8]

As this impassioned plea for rights suggests,
the freedmen doubted they would receive the equal
treatment they were entitled to after the Civil War.
They quickly realized that it is one thing to have
rights on paper and quite another to enjoy them in
practice.

With African-Americans attending all the
constitutional conventions called in response to the
Reconstruction Act of 1867, white Southerners were
deprived of control at those conventions and later in
state and local governments both as a result of the
large number of African-American voters and
because many ex-Confederates were disqualified
from holding office or voting until they met specific
requirements outlined by the President and Congress. Lacking the legal means to keep African-
Americans from voting, white Southerners resorted
to illegal means to intimidate African-Americans,
especially those who voted and held office. The best
known of these was the Ku Klux Klan, which began
making nightly raids in 1867.

The Klan used terror to keep African-Americans from exercising their new rights as citizens,
perhaps most importantly their right to vote.

Lynching became common. A whole generation of
black leadership was suppressed or slain. [9] In
addition to feeling the brutality of the Ku Klux Klan's
actions and daily threats of violence, African-
Americans were now threatened with economic
hardship, the loss of employment and income, if they
voted.

Despite these obstacles in their path, African-
Americans persisted in voting. They saw the
postwar Republican Party as the champion of
African-American voting and citizenship rights. The
attitudes of Democrats in Congress were perceived
as less favorable. For this reason, more and more
African-Americans gave their political allegiance to
the Republican Party. But although the majority of
African-Americans voted Republican, a small
number of African-Americans across the country did
support the Democrats. These Democratic supporters tended to be barbers, house servants, coachmen,
and artisans who voted as their employers did either
from sympathy or from fear. Other politically
conscious African-Americans left the Republican
Party for their own reasons, but Republican presidential candidate Ulysses S. Grant clearly owed his
1868 election victory in part to the votes of thousands
of newly enfranchised blacks. [10]

The Republican Party continued to pledge its
support to African-Americans who represented
badly needed votes. As time passed, however, it
became apparent that the Republicans were only
paying lip service to the African-American cause.
While in office, Grant did very little to help African-
Americans despite his Party's campaign promises.
For instance, Congress passed laws to suppress
violence and proclaim martial law if southern state
officials could not or would not carry out Reconstruction policies, many of which benefited African-
Americans. Although the Grant administration
theoretically supported the laws, it did little to
enforce them.

Between 1868 and 1870, southern African-
Americans actually gained an electoral majority:
703,000 African-Americans were qualified to vote
while only 627,000 whites were. Beverly Nash, a

South Carolina legislator, expressed the optimism of the newly enfranchised African-Americans:

.... We are not prepared for this suffrage. But we can learn. Give a man tools and let him commence to use them, and in time he will learn a trade. So it is with voting. We may not understand it at first, but in time we shall learn to do our duty. [11]

And learn to do their duty they did. As a result of the number of southern African-Americans who voted, twenty-two African-Americans from the South served in Congress between 1870 and 1901,

Bettmann Archive

R E · C O N S T R U C T I O N,
OR "A WHITE MAN'S GOVERNMENT".

Currier & Ives lithograph 1868

two of them as senators. But the new-found political power of southern African-Americans was lost almost as soon as it was won.

FEDERAL AMBIVALENCE

Whites came to consider the Reconstruction reforms and African-American advances in political equality as privileges temporarily bestowed on African-Americans. Few southern whites recognized the

Republican governments or African-American elected officials controlling their states. The old-line Democrats stood ready to reinstate their own leaders and to see that the African-Americans once ousted, would "stay in their place." [12]

Only the presence of federal troops at the polls made it possible for African-Americans to vote at all. The fate of the southern freedmen was finally sealed as part of the political "deal" that gave the 1876 presidential election to Rutherford B. Hayes. Southern Democrats agreed to throw their electoral votes behind Hayes when he promised to withdraw the last of the federal troops from the South. By 1876, only three southern states—Florida, Louisiana, and South Carolina—still had Reconstruction governments. Soon after Hayes took office in March 1877, the remaining garrisons were removed from Louisiana and South Carolina.

Hayes made several trips to the South, assuring African-Americans that their rights would be safer in southern hands than in the control of the federal government. This was not true. With no federal intervention, the programs for ensuring African-American participation in government stopped abruptly. States began to change their constitutions to disenfranchise African-Americans, relegating them to positions of social and political second-class citizenship. The withdrawal of troops by President Hayes marked the abandonment, not only of Reconstruction, but of African-Americans. The North, preoccupied with its own rising industrialism and with the development of the West, was willing to allow the white South to solve its race problems without federal intervention.

The era of Reconstruction was generally coming to a close. In many places it was over by 1872. With the passage of the Amnesty Act of 1872, all but the most prominent ex-Confederates were again permitted to vote and southern whites regained control of their state governments. They began to search for ways to neutralize African-American political power and to disenfranchise African-Americans that would not be declared unconstitutional. However, this task was complex, for these new legislators sought to restrict the voting rights of African-Americans without denying poor whites their rights, while staying within the legal constraints of the U.S. Constitution.

For many, violence was still the surest means to accomplish this task. In countless communities, African-Americans faced severe reprisals if they appeared in town on election day. Polling places were frequently located far from African-American communities, roads were blocked, and bridges and ferries necessary to reach polling places were conveniently out of service at election time. Polling locations were sometimes moved without notifying African-American voters; or if they were notified, election officials thought nothing of making a last minute decision not to change the place after all.

When it was to their advantage though, white planters made sure that their African-American workers were able to exercise their right to vote. Manipulation of those African-Americans who were permitted to vote was not uncommon. Politicians would woo African-American voters throughout the campaigns and on election eve would hold parties for black voters, with plenty of food and whiskey, to remind them to vote for their benefactors.

Election laws were also so imperfect that in many communities uniform ballots were not required, and officials winked at Democrats who cast several ballots. Ballot box stuffing was so widespread that South Carolina passed an "Eight Ballot Law," which required that ballots for different offices be dropped into different ballot boxes. Ballots dropped into the wrong box were not counted. Meanwhile, areas with heavy concentrations of African-Americans were broken up by a system of gerrymandering that rendered the African-American vote ineffective.

Disenfranchisement of African-Americans became easier when, in 1883, the U.S. Supreme Court declared the Civil Rights Act of 1875, (which had opened public areas to everyone, regardless of color) unconstitutional. Then, in 1884, Grover Cleveland became the first Democrat since pre-Civil War days

to occupy the White House. He favored giving back to the southern states the captured flags of the Confederacy, a policy indicative of his administrative posture. However, Cleveland did appoint some African-Americans to federal offices in the South. By 1888 Benjamin Harrison regained the Presidency for the Republicans. Once again, some African-Americans were named to public office, but primarily as a means of appeasing the entire race to prevent further trouble. In issues of great and far-reaching importance to African-Americans, neither Republicans nor Democrats came to the African-American population's aid. Congress defeated all civil rights measures.

DISCRIMINATION AT THE POLLS

In 1890, the first legislation establishing "literacy" tests as a prerequisite to voting was adopted in Mississippi. The same year, Mississippi's constitution was revised with the obvious purpose of disenfranchising African-Americans.

A suffrage amendment was written which imposed a poll tax of two dollars, excluded voters convicted of bribery, burglary, theft, arson, perjury, murder and bigamy, and also barred all who could not read any section of the state constitution, or understand it when read, or give a reasonable interpretation of it. [13]

The **literacy tests**, which required voters to be able to read, were applied in a blatantly discriminatory fashion. A joke that was widespread during this time concerned a Mississippi registrar who, confronted by a Harvard-educated African-American who could read not only English but also Latin and Greek, rejected him when he was unable to read a section of a Chinese newspaper. Testing was left to the discretion of the registrar. Needless to say there were no African-American registrars. The assumption was that white registrars would usually hold African-Americans strictly to the law but would overlook the deficiencies of whites.

The Democratic Party also worked to deter African-Americans from voting. As the Party became more firmly entrenched in the South, it was able to restrict participation in its primaries to whites, rendering African-American political power virtually nonexistent. Further, the Democratic Party felt threatened by a possible political alliance between the Republicans and another party, the Populists or people's party, which was the political agency of the farmers. In 1892, the Populists sought to win the African-American vote in most of the southern states and to unseat the Democrats. Recognizing the potential political power of the sheer numbers of African-Americans in the South, the Populists sought desperately to secure the franchise for African-Americans in areas where they had been barred from voting for more than a decade. The threat of an alliance between the Populists and Republicans led the southern Democratic Party first to work for general African-American disenfranchisement, then to turn to the African-American voters for their support.

In some communities, African-Americans were soon being coerced to vote for Democrats by the very people who once had dared them to vote at all. Many African-Americans, however, remained loyal to the Populists, who advocated political and social equality, but in spite of the African-American vote, the Populists failed to unseat the Democrats.

The 1890s also saw the establishment of the **Poll Tax**, a fee that had to be paid before a person could vote in Mississippi, South Carolina, and other states. For example, in 1895 South Carolina adopted the following voting requirements: "two years' residence, a poll tax of $1, the ability to read and write the constitution, or to own property worth $300.00, and the disqualification of convicts."[14]

The fees were prohibitive to the many African-Americans who had no property and were not paid a fair wage; they also prevented poor whites from voting. If a person did not pay the tax, or if he lost the receipt showing payment, he was not allowed to vote. Indeed, many unscrupulous politicians capitalized on the inability of African-Americans to pay the tax by providing the fee to those African-Americans who agreed to vote for them. As late as 1937, the constitutionality of the poll tax was tested and upheld by the U.S. Supreme Court. Not until the passage of the Twenty-fourth Amendment in 1964 was the poll tax finally ruled unconstitutional:

The right of citizens of the United States to vote in any primary or other election for President or Vice-President, for electors for President or Vice-President, or for Senator or Representative in Congress, shall not be denied or abridged by the United States or any State by reason of failure to pay any poll tax or other tax.

In 1896, the *Plessy v. Ferguson* Supreme Court decision established the "separate but equal" doctrine. The Court's decision that segregation did not violate the Thirteenth and Fourteenth Amendments in effect gave state officials the license to segregate public places, including the polls. This practice was a major setback in the progress African-Americans had made toward obtaining equality and voting rights. The Supreme Court's decision in *Plessy v. Ferguson* validated the segregationist practices of the South, and it was to serve as the basis for laws until 1954, when it would at long last be overturned by the *Brown v. Topeka Board of Education* decision.

Meanwhile, discriminatory practices and legislation sank to even further depths of unfairness.

In 1898 Louisiana designed and wrote into its constitution the **"Grandfather" Clause** which deprived African-Americans of the right to vote by limiting voter registration to those citizens whose fathers or grandfathers had voted before 1867. Certainly most African-Americans were excluded, since most of them had been slaves until 1865 and had not been given full citizenship rights until 1868. At the same time, the clause served as a loophole that allowed poor whites to retain their right to vote if they failed the literacy test or could not pay the poll tax.[15] Eighteen years would pass before the U.S. Supreme Court declared the Grandfather Clause unconstitutional.

Poll tax requirements, elaborate and confusing election and balloting procedures, highly decentralized election codes (in which administration was left to the discretion of local officials) and violence were the primary measures used to disenfranchise African-Americans. By the turn of the century, the number of African-Americans who were voting had decreased by as much as 60 to 80 percent, particularly in the South: every former Confederate state had successfully disenfranchised the African-American man by 1910. [16] Most Northerners at this point generally thought it unwise to force the issue of African-American suffrage on the South, believing that outside interference would make Southerners defensive. And so George H. White of North Carolina was to be the last African-American Congressman of this once hopeful era. White left Congress in 1901. By 1902 not a single southern African-American legislator was serving at the state or the national level.

African-Americans eventually surmounted the barriers that had been erected to prevent their participation in the political process. Their success was due in large part to the emergence of several organizations that focused on removing the voting and citizenship restrictions that had developed since the passage of the Reconstruction Amendments.

VOTER RIGHTS ORGANIZATIONS

The early 1900s saw the rise of organizations committed to obtaining full rights of citizenship, including the right to vote, for African-Americans. The Niagara Movement, the National Association for the Advancement of Colored People (NAACP), the Urban League, and the Congress on Racial Equality were among these groups.

THE NIAGARA MOVEMENT

In 1905, the **Niagara Movement** was formed. Dr. William Edward Burghardt (W.E.B.) DuBois, its founder and developer, gathered the leading African-American intellectuals of the time at Niagara Falls,

Canada. They were dedicated to the promotion of the following stated principles:

-freedom of speech and criticism
-an unfettered press
-manhood suffrage
-abolition of all caste distinctions based upon race and color
-recognition of human brotherhood as a practical and present creed
-recognition of the highest and best human training
-as the monopoly of no class or race
-a belief in the dignity of labor
-united effort to realize these ideas under wise and courageous leadership[17]

The Niagara Movement planned a more militant attack against discrimination than those of the previous century. At its first conference, the Movement issued a declaration of principles that stated: "We believe that Negroes should protest emphatically and continuously against the curtailment of their political rights." [18] The refusal of accommodations to these African-American leaders on the New York side of Niagara Falls only confirmed the urgency of their mission.

The group demanded equal economic opportunity, equal education, fair administration of justice, and an end to segregation. Branches were formed throughout the country and annual meetings held at sites historically important to African-Americans. Besides holding public meetings, The Niagara Movement submitted articles to newspapers and petitioned state legislatures as a means of attracting attention to their message. Criticism by the press and lack of money continued to plague the organization's efforts. It remained small and received little white support, but the Niagara Movement did succeed in making the public more aware of African-Americans' discontent.

The movement finally gained white support when in August of 1908, a bloody race riot occurred in Springfield, Illinois, sparked by a white woman's claim that she had been molested by an African-American man. The charge later proved false, but the woman's confession would came too late to avert the violence. In the riot's wake, William English Walling, a reporter who covered the event, called for an end to racial attacks. He and a group of other white reformers invited DuBois and the Niagara Movement to join forces with them. In 1908, the Niagara Movement held its last meeting at Oberlin, Ohio, where its members voted to join Walling and form an integrated organization, the National Association for the Advancement of Colored People (NAACP).

THE NATIONAL ASSOCIATION FOR THE ADVANCEMENT OF COLORED PEOPLE (NAACP)

The founding meeting of the **NAACP** was held on February 12, 1909. It was attended by a number of distinguished Americans, black and white. Among them were the eminent clergymen Francis Grimke and Alexander Walters, both champions of African-American rights; social reformer Jane Addams, the founder of Chicago's Hull House; novelist and literary critic William Dean Howells; educator John Dewey; the crusading editor and publisher of the New York *Evening Post* (and grandson of abolitionist William Lloyd Garrison), Oswald Garrison Vilard, and W.E.B. DuBois.

The first official meeting was held in 1910; with the exception of DuBois, the first officers elected were all whites. The organization set as its mission an attack on racial discrimination and emphasized redress through court action. The NAACP was to bring about changes for African-Americans in voting, housing, interstate travel, public accommodations, and school desegregation. It would accomplish these things by operating on the legal and congressional fronts; the NAACP also published *The Crisis*, a national magazine that presented facts on injustices to the public, encouraged the efforts of African-American writers and poets to illuminate these matters, and used its Legal Redress Committee

and investigators to uncover illegal acts of racial discrimination.

The NAACP sought to achieve:
-the end of lynching and lawlessness against blacks
-increased police protection for blacks
-voting rights for all citizens
-increased black participation in industry
-just defense of blacks in court
-the end of segregation in all its forms.[19]

The NAACP lobbied for the passage of an anti-lynching law in Congress in 1921. Although the law passed the House, it did not pass the Senate, and died.

THE URBAN LEAGUE

In 1910, Dr. George E. Haynes and other reformers, both African-American and white, organized the **National Urban League**. Haynes believed that racial harmony would lead to an improvement in the quality of life for both races. While a graduate student at Columbia University, he had conducted a study of the social and economic conditions of African-Americans in New York City. The data Haynes gathered were placed at the disposal of the National League for the Protection of Colored Women and the Committee for Improving Industrial Conditions of Negroes in New York. These organizations were so moved by the findings that they established an agency that would coordinate a program for the improvement of African-American community life in New York.

In 1911, the three groups merged to form the National League of Urban Conditions Among Negroes, which would become known as the National Urban League. Haynes and Eugene Kinckle Jones served as the executive officers of the newly formed organization. The League's mission was to open new opportunities for African-Americans in industry and to assist transplanted rural African-Americans in adjusting to urban areas. It

Chicago, Ill.: A group of Negroes, from Tennessee's Fayette County, stand outside one of the tents they set up on Chicago's South Side August 16th. This is part of a traveling group who will stage a series of demonstrations designed to help "resolve racial wars." The group of Tenant Farmers, Share Croppers and Day Workers said they were evicted from their homes by White Landlords when they tried to register and vote. The baby, Freeman Clemon, six-months-old, (foreground) was born in a tent city at Mason, Tenn. The others are not identified. 8/21/61

sought to improve health, housing, recreation, and job opportunities for African-Americans who lived in the cities. While the NAACP focused on voting rights, the Urban League focused on economic and social conditions.

Although all of the organizations dedicated to ensuring full citizenship rights for African-Americans were effective, additional measures were needed before African-Americans could finally enjoy the vote.

THE VOTER EDUCATION PROJECT

During the 50-year period between 1911 and 1961, the NAACP and Urban League were the most visible national organizations committed to attaining civil rights and voting rights for African-Americans. Local efforts were also mounted, but the national efforts were more widely publicized.

Another organization rose to prominence in 1961. The **Southern Regional Conference**, a biracial group based in Atlanta, drew attention with its **Voter Education Project**, a multi-state effort to ensure African-Americans the right to vote freely in the South. The Project won the support of major civil rights groups and was endorsed by both the Democratic and Republican National Committees. Its activities spanned eleven southern states, with participating local and national agencies conducting the Project programs designed to register African-Americans to vote. Program reports were then submitted to the Voter Education Project for analysis, and the information was distributed nationally.

Through a combination of support for locally initiated voter registration efforts and the initiation of its own voter registration drives, the Project assumed the major responsibility for fulfilling the promise of the Voting Rights Act of 1965. More than a million African-American citizens became registered voters between 1965 and 1969. As more African-Americans were elected, the Project worked to educate African-American officeholders on the intricacies of vital issues and techniques to obtain appropriations important to African-American voters. More new schools, paved streets, and police protection for neglected African-American neighborhoods were the result.[20]

MARTIN LUTHER KING JR. IN SELMA

Despite the work of voters' rights organizations and existing civil rights legislation hundreds of thousands of African-Americans in the South were still being deterred from voting. During the summer and fall of 1964, the Council of Federated Organizations—an association of the major civil rights organizations, the National Council of Churches, and other groups—encountered tremendous opposition in its drive to increase voter registration of African-Americans. Even after the 1964 Presidential election of Lyndon Johnson, who was committed to civil rights, they continued to face bitter opposition.

Southern whites, especially in areas where the African-American population was large, appeared more opposed to voter registration drives than to the demonstrations for desegregated public accommodations then taking place: better to share a washroom than a polling booth, where community decisions were made.

In early 1965, Dr. Martin Luther King, Jr., organized a large-scale voting rights drive that was scheduled to culminate in a protest march from Selma to Montgomery, Alabama. The march was to dramatize the denial of voting rights to African-Americans who had tried to register in Selma.

UPI

Belzoni, Miss: A group of Negroes raise their hands as they take an oath during a voter registration drive 6/18. Memphis to Jackson freedom marchers camped here 6/18 night and staged a march on the Post Office where they urged local Negroes to register and vote. 6/19/66

18

Washington: President Johnson shakes hands with The Rev. Martin Luther King after handing him a pen during the signing of the Civil Rights bill into law during a White House ceremony. 7/2/1964

Cleveland Public Library-UPI

Capturing national TV coverage and newspaper headlines, the historic march was set to take place on March 7, 1965. But on that day 200 Alabama state troopers and deputies of the Dallas County sheriff's office halted the 525 African-American marchers by charging into their ranks with tear gas, nightsticks, and whips in what was seen by many observers as a last-ditch effort to enforce Governor George Wallace's order banning the demonstration. Sixty-seven African-Americans were injured and seventeen were hospitalized. Television cameras covered the event, and viewers across the nation saw the police brutality waged on the unarmed and peaceful marchers.

The next day, March 8, Governor George Wallace denied that the police had made an intemperate display of force. The march was rescheduled. On March 9, President Johnson stated that he was certain that all Americans

joined in deploring the brutality with which a number of black citizens of Alabama were treated when they sought to dramatize their deep and sincere interest in obtaining the right to vote. [21]

On this same day Federal Judge Frank M. Johnson, Jr., issued a restraining order to permit the march. Even with this ruling, the marchers were turned back a second time.

President Johnson recognized the clear need for additional legislation to protect the rights of voters. Public outrage and the realization that African-American votes had helped elect him led Johnson to demand a new voting rights act from Congress:

EXCERPTS FROM JOHNSON'S SPEECH TO CONGRESS - March 15, 1965

All Americans must have the privileges of citizenship regardless of race. And they are going to have those privileges of citizenship regardless of race.

But I would like to caution you and remind you that to exercise these privileges takes much more than legal right. It requires a trained mind and a healthy body. It requires a decent home, and the chance to find a job, and the opportunity to escape from the clutches of poverty.

Of course people cannot contribute to the Nation if they are never taught to read or write, if their bodies are stunted from hunger, if their sickness goes untended, if their life is spent in hopeless poverty just drawing a welfare check.

So we want to open the gates to opportunity. But we are also going to give all our people — black and white — the help that they need to walk through those gates.

• • •

In this same month 95 years ago — on March 30, 1870 — the Constitution of the United States was amended for the 15th time to guarantee that no citizen of our land should be denied the right to vote because of race or color.

• • •

. . . I speak tonight for the dignity of man and the destiny of democracy.

I urge every member of both parties — Americans of all religions and of all colors — from every section of this country — to join me in that cause.

At times history and fate meet at a single time in a single place to shape a turning point in man's unending search for freedom. So it was at Lexington and Concord. So it was a century ago at Appomattox. So it was last week in Selma, Ala.

There, long-suffering men and women peacefully protested the denial of their rights as Americans. Many were brutally assaulted. One good man — a man of God — was killed.

There was no cause for pride in what has happened in Selma.

There is no cause for self-satisfaction in the long denial of equal rights for millions of Americans.

But there is cause for hope and for faith in our democracy in what is happening here tonight.

For the cries of pain, and the hymns and protests of oppressed people, have summoned into convocation all the majesty of this great Government, the Government of the greatest Nation on earth.

Our mission is at once the oldest and most basic of this country: to right wrong, to do justice, to serve man.

• • •

This was the first nation in the history of the world to be founded with a purpose. The great phrases of that purpose still sound in every American heart, north and south: "All men are created equal" — "Government by consent of the governed" — "Give me liberty or give me death."...

Those words are a promise to every citizen that he shall share in the dignity of man. This dignity cannot be found in man's possessions. It cannot be found in his power or in his position. It really rests on his right to be treated as a man equal in opportunity to all others. It says that he shall share in freedom, he shall choose his leaders, educate his children, provide for his family according to his ability and his merits as a human being.

To apply any other test — to deny a man his hopes because of his color or race or his religion or the place of his birth — is not only to do injustice, it is to deny America and to dishonor the dead who gave their lives for American freedom.

• • •

. . . But about this there can and should be no argument. Every American citizen must have an equal right to vote. . . .

Yet the harsh fact is that in many places in this country men and women are kept from voting simply because they are Negroes.

Every device of which human ingenuity is capable has been used to deny this right. The Negro citizen may go to register only to be told that the day is wrong, or the hour is late, or the official in charge is absent.

And if he persists, and if he manages to present himself to the registrar, he may be disqualified because he did not spell out his middle name or because he abbreviated a word on the application.

And if he manages to fill out an application he is given a test. The registrar is the sole judge of whether he passes this test. He may be asked to recite the entire Constitution, or explain the most complex provisions of State law and even a college degree cannot be used to prove that he can read and write.

For the fact is that the only way to pass these barriers is to show a white skin.

•   •   •

. . . The Constitution says that no person shall be kept from voting because of his race or his color. We have all sworn an oath before God to support and to defend that Constitution.

We must now act in obedience to that oath.

Wednesday I will send to Congress a law designed to eliminate illegal barriers to the right to vote.

This bill will strike down restrictions to voting in all elections — Federal, State, and local — which have been used to deny Negroes the right to vote.

This bill will establish a simple, uniform standard which cannot be used however ingenious the effort to flout our Constitution.

It will provide for citizens to be registered by officials of the U.S. Government if the State officials refuse to register them.

It will eliminate tedious, unnecessary lawsuits which delay the right to vote.

Finally, this legislation will insure that properly registered individuals are not prohibited from voting.

•   •   •

To those who seek to avoid action by their National Government in their home communities — who want to and who seek to maintain purely local control over elections — the answer is simple.

Open your polling places to all your people.

Allow men and women to register and vote whatever the color of their skin.

Extend the rights of citizenship to every citizen of this land.

There is no constitutional issue here. The command of the Constitution is plain.

There is no moral issue. It is wrong — deadly wrong — to deny any of your fellow Americans the right to vote in this country.

There is no issue of States rights or National rights. There is only the struggle for human rights.

•   •   •

The bill that I am presenting to you will be known as a civil rights bill. But in a larger sense, most of the program I am recommending is a civil rights program. Its object is to open the city of hope to all people of all races.

Because all Americans just must have the right to vote. And we are going to give them that right. [22]

On March 17, 1965, Judge Johnson upheld the right of African-American demonstrators to march as originally planned and forbade Governor Wallace and other Alabama officials to intimidate the participants in any way. Furthermore, the judge ordered the governor to provide police protection for the march, and President Johnson called in the Alabama National Guard to protect the marchers.

The third attempt to stage the march successfully got under way on March 21, 1965. The 5-day, 54-mile march from Selma to Montgomery, Alabama, secured voting rights for African-Americans throughout the nation. On the final day of the march, the 300 demonstrators had been joined by some 35,000 supporters from all over the country.

THE VOTING RIGHTS ACT OF 1965

In his commencement address at Howard University on June 4, 1965, President Johnson said of the Voting Rights Act of 1965:

> *In far too many ways American Negroes have been another nation; deprived of freedom, crippled by hatred, the doors of opportunity closed to hope. In our time, change has come to this nation.... The voice of the Negro was the call to action.... The Voting Rights Bill will be the latest, and among the most important, in a long series of victories....But this victory...is not the end. But it is, perhaps, the end of the beginning.* [23]

Congress passed the **Voting Rights Act of 1965** with unusual swiftness. Signed into law by President Johnson on August 6, 1965, it authorized the Attorney General to send federal examiners to register African-American voters in locations where he concluded that local registrars were not registering African-American voters. The Act also empowered the Department of Justice to send federal agents to monitor elections. It suspended all literacy tests and other such requirements that impeded registration and voting in states and counties using them. The Act applied to all states and counties where less than 50 percent of the adults had voted in 1964.

Affected were Alabama, Georgia, Louisiana, Mississippi, South Carolina, Virginia, twenty-six counties in North Carolina, Alaska, and scattered counties in Arizona, Idaho, and Hawaii.

Despite opposition to the measure and charges by some African-Americans that Attorney General Nicholas Katzenbach did not send federal examiners quickly enough in response to alleged violations, the Voting Rights Act of 1965 was to be responsible for the most significant increase in the number of African-American votes since Reconstruction. The Act was also to prove effective in increasing the number of African-American office holders.

Canton, Miss: Federal voter registrar Louis Searson 8/10 fills out a form for a prospective Negro voter as dozens of other Negroes wait in line. Federal registration offices opened 8/10 here and in Greenwood, and others were expected later in other Mississippi counties. 8/10/65

UPI/Bettmann

EXCERPTS FROM "THE VOTING RIGHTS ACT OF 1965" PUBLIC LAW 89-11 0

Sec. 2. No voting qualification or prerequisite to voting, or standard, practice, or procedure shall be imposed or applied by any State or political subdivision to deny or abridge the right of any citizen of the United States to vote on account of race or color.

Sec.3. (b) If in a proceeding instituted by the Attorney General under any statute to enforce the guarantees of the fifteenth amendment in any State or political subdivision the court finds that a test or device has been used for the purpose or with the effect of denying or abridging the right of any citizen of the United States to vote on account of race or color, it shall suspend the use of tests and devices in such State or political subdivision as the court shall determine is appropriate and for such period as it deems necessary.

•   •   •

Sec.4. (a) To assure that the right of citizens of the United States to vote is not denied or abridged on account of race or color, no citizen shall be denied the right to vote in any Federal, State, or local election because of his failure to comply with any test or device in any State ...

•   •   •

(e)(1) Congress hereby declares that to secure the rights under the fourteenth amendment of persons educated in American-flag schools in which the predominant classroom language was other than English, it is necessary to prohibit the States from conditioning the right to vote of such persons on ability to read, write, understand, or interpret any matter in the English language.

(2) No person who demonstrates that he has successfully completed the sixth primary grade in a public school in, or a private school accredited by, any State or territory, the District of Columbia, or the Commonwealth of Puerto Rico in which the predominant classroom language was other than English, shall be denied the right to vote in any Federal, State, or local election because of this inability to read, write, understand, or interpret any matter in the English language, except that in States in which State law provides that a different level of education is presumptive of literacy, he shall demonstrate that he has successfully completed an equivalent level of education in a public school in, or a private school accredited by, any State or territory, the District of Columbia, or the Commonwealth of Puerto Rico in which the predominant classroom language was other than English.

•   •   •

Sec.10. (a) The Congress finds that the requirement of the payment of a poll tax as a precondition to voting (i) precludes persons of limited means from voting or imposes unreasonable financial hardship upon such persons as a precondition to their exercise of the franchise, (ii) does not bear a reasonable relationship to any legitimate State interest in the conduct of elections, and (iii) in some areas has the purpose or effect of denying persons the right to vote because of race or color. Upon the basis of these findings, Congress declares that the constitutional right of citizens to vote is denied or abridged in some areas by the requirement of the payment of a poll tax as a precondition to voting.

(b) In the exercise of the powers of Congress under section 5 of the fourteenth amendment and section 2 of the fifteenth amendment, the Attorney General is authorized and directed to institute forthwith in the name of the United States such actions, including actions against States or political subdivisions, for declaratory judgment or injunctive relief against the enforcement of any requirement of the payment of a poll tax as a precondition to voting. . . . [24]

The Voting Rights Act has periodically been renewed in order to extend certain provisions as required. It has been expanded to include all minorities and has narrowed the gap between the philosophy of democracy in the United States and its reality for millions of Americans.

In the 1982 renewal, the following political areas were affected by the Voting Rights Act:

All of Alabama, Georgia, Louisiana, Mississippi, South Carolina, Virginia.

39 counties in North Carolina; 9 counties in Arizona; 2 in California (Monterey and Yuba); 1 in Idaho (Elmire); 3 in New York (Bronx, Kings, New York); 1 in Wyoming (Campbell). [25]

That the Act continues to affect different regions testifies to the need for continuing renewal.

SIGN POSTS ON THE ROAD TO AFRICAN-AMERICAN SUFFRAGE

1865 The Thirteenth Amendment abolishes slavery.

1865 The Fourteenth Amendment grants citizenship to African-Americans.

1870 The Fifteenth Amendment declares all citizens have the right to vote regardless of race, color, or previous conditions of servitude.

1875 The Civil Rights bill guarantees equal access to public places (declared unconstitutional in 1883).

1890 The first "literacy" tests are established to exclude blacks from voting in Mississippi.

1895 The first poll tax ($1) is levied in South Carolina.

1896 The U.S. Supreme Court's *Plessy v. Ferguson* decision establishes the "separate but equal" doctrine.

1905 W.E.B. DuBois founds the Niagara Movement.

1909 The National Association for the Advancement of Colored People (NAACP) is established.

1910 The National Urban League is organized.

1920 The Nineteenth Amendment grants all women the right to vote.

1928 The first African-American Congressman since Reconstruction (1865-77) is elected in Illinois. (Oscar DePriest)

1948 A Presidential Executive order desegregates the armed forces.

1954 The U.S. Supreme Court's *Brown v. Topeka Board of Education* decision orders school desegregation, reversing the Court's 1896 *Plessy v. Ferguson* decision.

1955 Civil Rights workers organize the Montgomery, Alabama, bus boycott.

1957 The Southern Christian Leadership Conference (SCLC) is founded. The Civil Rights Act of 1957 enforces the Fifteenth Amendment and gives the Justice Department the power to bring suit on behalf of African-Americans deprived of their voting rights.

1960 Congress passes the Voter Registration Act.

1961 The Voter Education Project, (1961-63) is inaugurated. The Justice Department brings 45 voting suits, compared with 10 in the previous three years of the Eisenhower administration.

1963 The Civil Rights March on Washington. Martin Luther King, Jr. makes his "I have a Dream" speech.

1964 The Civil Rights Act of 1964 forbids segregation in transportation and places of public accommodation throughout the U.S.

1964 The Twenty-Fourth Amendment prohibits the use of poll tax as a qualification for voting in federal elections.

1965 The Voting Rights Act of 1965 authorizes the U.S. Attorney General to suspend the use of "literacy" tests to prevent African-Americans from voting.

1966 The U.S. Supreme Court rules the poll tax unlawful in all elections.

1966 The first African-American since Reconstruction is elected to the U.S. Senate, from Massachusetts. (Edward Brooke)

1967 The first African-American is appointed to the United States Supreme Court. (Thurgood Marshall)

1967 The first African-American mayor is elected from a major American city. (Carl B. Stokes, Cleveland)

1968 The Rev. Martin Luther King, Jr. is assassinated.

1969 The first African-American woman to serve in the United States House of Representatives is elected. (Shirley Chisholm, New York)

1969 The first African-American mayor of a biracial southern city since Reconstruction is elected. (Charles Evers, Fayette, Mississippi)

1970 The Voting Rights Act of 1965 is renewed and expanded to include the reduction of residency requirements for voting.

1971 The Twenty-Sixth Amendment lowers the voting age to 18.

1972 The first African-American woman to run for President of the United States in Democratic primaries. (Shirley Chisholm)

1973 The first African-American woman from a southern state to serve in Congress is elected. (Barbara Jordan, Texas)

1982 The Voting Rights Act is renewed.

1984 The first African-American man runs for President of the United States by seeking the Democratic nomination. (Jesse Jackson)

1986 Martin Luther King, Jr. Day is established, the first national holiday honoring an African-American.

The road to equality was paved by votes.
Voting changed the past and it will shape the future.

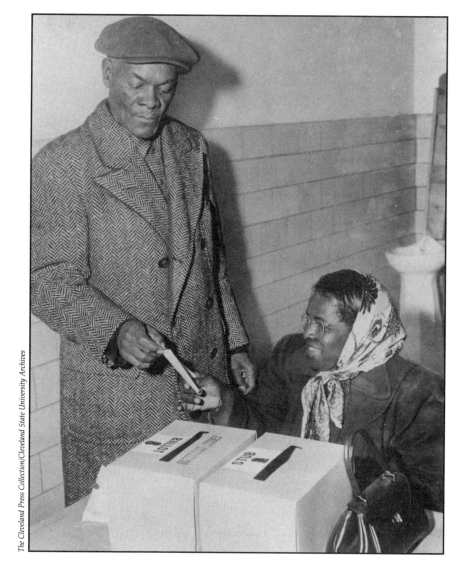

"Our whole campaign...has been centered around the right to vote."

SETBACKS AND ADVANCES: AFRICAN-AMERICANS DISCOVER THE POWER OF THE VOTE

As the march toward African-American suffrage entered the twentieth century, it met with many obstacles and setbacks. By the beginning of the century it seemed that African-Americans would make no further gains. The process of depriving African-Americans of the vote had been effective in the years since the Reconstruction: the departure of North Carolina's George H. White from Congress in 1901 seemed to signal the end of progress and the beginning of a new period of retrenchment.

By 1910, African-Americans had been disenfranchised by state constitutional provisions in North Carolina, Alabama, Virginia, Georgia, and Oklahoma. Where they were not denied the vote by law, African-Americans were often denied the vote by practices like those described in Chapter One. In the early 1900's, African-Americans were seen by many as aliens whose ignorance, poverty, and racial inferiority were incompatible with the logical and orderly process of government. Throughout the South the disenfranchisement of African-Americans was hailed as a constructive act of statesmanship.

Ironically, the coming of war — first World War I and later World War II — opened the doors of economic opportunity for African-Americans, as northern industries geared up for battle. With this opportunity came new hopes for greater political power. Those African-Americans who fought honorably in defense of their country in World Wars I and II would still be denied their rights as citizens. Black men who had gone to war "to make the world safe for democracy" came home to discover that they still did not enjoy the equality and rights that American democracy stood for.[1]

But the new residential patterns that developed from African-American migration to the north during this era brought about new concentrations of African-American political power, giving them a political strength they had not had since Reconstruction. African-Americans were soon back in the thick of American politics. Another development was also to have a far-reaching impact on the political landscape. In 1920 the Nineteenth Amendment was passed, giving African-American women the right to vote along with all other American women.

AFRICAN-AMERICAN VOICES IN CONGRESS

In 1928, the large numbers of politically active African-Americans in Chicago helped Oscar DePriest win election to the House of Representatives, making him the first African-American Congressman since Reconstruction. DePriest, also the first African-American ever to be elected from a northern state, was born in Florence, Alabama. Moving to the West and then to the North as a child, he studied business and bookkeeping. Finally settling in Chicago in 1889, he became a painter and master decorator and amassed a fortune in real estate and the stock market before deciding to enter politics. DePriest was elected a Cook County Commissioner in 1904. In 1908 he was appointed an alternate delegate to the Republican National Convention and in 1915 became Chicago's first African-American Alderman. In 1928, he declared himself a candidate for the post of Republican committeeman for the Third Ward. But when Martin B. Madden, an Illinois Republican Congressman, died suddenly, DePriest switched tracks and campaigned successfully for the vacant Congressional seat.

In a speech made the following year, he urged African-Americans to vote, pointing out that African-Americans would never make substantial progress until they elected political leaders who would fight for African-American interests in Congress. Although he officially represented only his own district, DePriest was seen by many as representing all African-Americans in the United States. During his three terms in office, he was in great demand as a speaker and was pointed to by African-Americans everywhere as the realization of their dream. One African-American newspaper of the time said DePriest's presence in Washington gave African-Americans "new hope, new courage, and new inspiration." Not surprisingly, many whites were alarmed that an African-American had achieved so high a distinction in American politics. DePriest's wife was shunned at many of Washington's social functions, to the point where many white politicians' wives refused to attend the political wives' luncheons if she was going to be there, but the DePriests were not deterred from their mission.[2]

In 1934, DePriest was defeated by Arthur Mitchell, who became the first African-American Democrat to sit in Congress. Mitchell had won Democratic approval only after Harry Baker, who had defeated him in the primary, died suddenly, leaving the Republican DePriest without a challenger. Aided by the growing support of African-Americans for Franklin Roosevelt and the Democrats in the mid-1930's, Mitchell managed to unseat DePriest by just 3,000 votes. His victory signaled

what was to become the first major shift in African-American voting sentiment since Reconstruction.

Arthur Mitchell had been born to former slaves in 1883 in Chambers County, Alabama. He was well educated, having attended Tuskegee Institute and Columbia and Harvard Universities. By 1929, he had already made his own mark as the founder of Armstrong Agricultural School in West Butler, Alabama. He was to become a wealthy landowner and a lawyer with a thriving practice in Washington, D.C.

One of Congressman Mitchell's achievements was the elimination of the notorious "Jim Crow" railroad car.

On a trip to Hot Springs, Arkansas, on the Chicago and Rock Island Railroad, he had been forced to ride in a Jim Crow car. Mitchell brought a lawsuit against the railroad in 1937, challenging the constitutionality of the practice that had forced him to leave his first-class accommodations for inferior ones. In 1941, the United States Supreme Court declared such Jim Crow practices illegal in interstate travel.

Both Mitchell and DePriest also fought to eliminate the poll tax. Though not all of their struggles were successful, they laid the groundwork for eventual legislative triumphs. For, apart from their importance in Congress as voices for the African-American cause, the two Congressmen served as a bridge between African-American and white liberals, an alliance that was to win the later civil rights victories of the 1960s.

Throughout the 1920s and early 1930s, most African-Americans remained Republicans. However, after Franklin D. Roosevelt was elected President in 1932, growing numbers of African-Americans began to vote Democratic, as the 1934 election of Mitchell suggests. The great majority of African-Americans continue to vote Democratic today.

Roosevelt's Republican predecessor, Herbert Hoover, who had gained the Presidency in 1928, had hurt many African-Americans with his support of the so-called southern Republican "lily-white" movement. He had further alienated African-Americans by his actions in two separate incidents. When African-Americans were excluded from the construction crews on the Boulder Dam project, at a time when their unemployment rate was far higher than that of whites, Hoover had remained silent. His nomination of John J. Parker, a North Carolinian, for the United States Supreme Court had added insult to injury. Judge Parker had locally opposed the participation of African-Americans in politics on the grounds that they were not deserving of such a right. Black leaders were furious over the appointment of such a man to the highest court in the land. The NAACP worked effectively for the defeat of members of the Senate who had voted to confirm the appointment.

Despite these incidents, however, most African-Americans continued to vote Republican. Seventy-five percent supported Hoover in 1932, the year he was defeated by Franklin D. Roosevelt. Roosevelt's administration was to show a greater degree of sensitivity to the needs of African-Americans than had previous administrations. As the Depression deepened and African-Americans increasingly came to feel that the Democratic platform addressed their needs more than that of the Republican Party, the African-American voting pattern switched from "Lincoln and Liberty" to "Roosevelt and Relief." African-Americans were to be instrumental in re-electing Roosevelt in 1936, with an estimated 80 to 90 percent of African-Americans casting their votes for FDR. [3] The loss of African-American loyalty to the Republican Party was one of the most significant political developments of modern U.S. history.

FDR'S "BLACK CABINET"

During Roosevelt's administration many African-Americans were appointed to high level jobs. These African-American advisors to the President were referred to as the "Black Cabinet." Some of its members and their positions were:

● ●

Mary McLeod Bethune	Director of the Division of the Negro Affairs of the National Youth Administration
Edgar Brown	Advisor of Negro Affairs in the Civilian Conservation Corps.
Crystal Bird Fauset	Racial Relations Advisor in the Office of Civilian Defense
William H. Hastie	Assistant Solicitor in the Department of the Interior
Frank S. Horne	Federal Housing Program Advisor
Colonel Campbell Johnson	Assistant to Head of the National Selective Service
Lawrence A. Oxley	Chief of the Division of Negro Labor in the Department of Labor
Tom Poston	Racial Advisor in the Office of War Information
William J. Trent	Racial Advisor in the Department of the Interior, later in the Federal Works Agency as the Racial Relations Officer
Robert L. Van	Special Assistant to the Attorney General
Robert C. Weaver	Racial Advisor in the Department of the Interior for the Federal Housing Authority

● ●

The Black Cabinet eventually numbered 100 federal appointees. For the most part, they did not have backgrounds as politicians. But this did not stop white administrators such as Secretary of the Interior Harold L. Ickes, a former president of the Chicago NAACP, from hiring racial advisors in the early days of the New Deal. The advisors' task was to press for economic and political equality of African-Americans.

THE WAR COMES HOME

World War II changed the social, political, and economic fabric of American society. African-Americans made a number of significant gains, both during the war and after; the disturbing parallels between the rhetoric of white supremacists in the U.S. and Hitler's doctrine of the master race could not be ignored. Throughout the 1940s, NAACP lawyers battled in the courts against school segregation and laws that deprived African-Americans living in the South of their right to vote. The political strength African-Americans were gaining during this period was being seen not only in the consideration both major parties gave them in national elections, but also in their own success in state and local elections.

In 1944 the Supreme Court banned the so-called "white primary," ruling that voting rights were "not to be nullified by a state through casting its electoral process in a form that permits a private organization (the Democratic Party) to practice racial discrimination in elections." [4] Profound anti-African-American sentiment still existed however, as a 1946 notice taped to a church door in response to this decision attests. "THE FIRST NIGGER WHO VOTES IN GEORGIA," it proclaimed, " WILL BE A DEAD NIGGER." [5]

Founded at the end of World War II, the United Nations also advocated racial equality, including in its charter a pledge of "universal respect for and observance of human rights and fundamental freedoms for all, without distinction of race, sex, language or religion...." making the gulf between the ideals of democracy and the realities of Jim Crow more painful than ever for African-American veterans returning to the United States. Walter White of the NAACP summarized the feeling of the time when he said that "either the Negro must obtain full citizenship status with all the rights and obligations thereby involved...or the democratic process for all America will be made meaningless." [6]

In 1948, Democratic President Harry Truman took decisive action to promote racial equality when he issued Presidential Executive Order 9981, which desegregated the armed forces and thus abolished many outrageous racist practices in the military. He also urged Congress to abolish once and for all the pernicious poll tax, enforce fair voting and hiring practices, and end Jim Crow practices in interstate transportation. In protest, four southern states subsequently restored the Republican Party to office.

By 1950, only about 25 percent of all African-Americans were registered voters, and the vast majority of those lived in the North. Most now were loyal Democrats. When Eisenhower was elected President in 1952, he received only 21 percent of the African-American vote. The Eisenhower administration did not press for civil rights and the federal courts thus began to take the lead in this area.[7] Eisenhower, however, did send federal troops in support of school desegregation in Little Rock, Arkansas.

THE CIVIL RIGHTS ACT OF 1957

The NAACP continued to challenge the concept of "separate but equal" in the courts. This ongoing struggle got a boost in the form of the Civil Rights Act of 1957, which was designed to overcome the disparity between the percentages of African-American and white registered voters and to enforce the original intent of the Fifteenth Amendment. The Act's key provision gave the U.S. Department of Justice the power to bring suit on behalf of African-Americans who had been denied their voting rights.

The 1957 legislation was the first civil rights act passed since Reconstruction: the Civil Rights Bill of 1875 had guaranteed equal access to public places, but had been declared unconstitutional in 1883. The 1957 Civil Rights Act was designed to remove the legal barriers still in force in southern states that disenfranchised African-Americans. Additional voting rights legislation followed in 1965. The Civil Rights Act was renewed in 1960, 1964, 1966, 1968, 1970, 1972, and 1988.

In 1990 the Act was again presented for amendment. The amendments proposed were designed to restore job protections for women and minorities that a series of Supreme Court decisions had weakened during the 1980s, making it more difficult to sue employers for discrimination. Congress passed the amended Act, but President Bush vetoed it on the grounds that it would lead to hiring quotas. The Senate failed by one vote to override the President's veto.[8] As this most recent struggle suggests, legislation intended to strengthen African-American civil and voting rights in recent decades has met with mixed success.

The raising of African-American political consciousness in the 1960s, however, made history of its own.

Approximately 8 million African-Americans voted in the 1964 presidential election, with 94 percent of the African-American vote going to Lyndon B. Johnson, who won in a landslide. [9] This enormous turnout demonstrated to politicians and society the impact the African-American vote could have on an election outcome.

This sharp rise in African-American political consciousness was due in part to the enthusiasm generated by the Civil Rights Movement in the South. A large increase in the turnout of African-American voters also resulted in a greater number of African-American Congressmen being elected in 1966. Major victories came in 1967 when African-Americans were elected to the office of mayor in two major cities—Carl B. Stokes in Cleveland, Ohio, and Richard Hatcher in Gary, Indiana. In both instances, it was organized African-American political strength that had made victory possible. In 1976, African-American voters would cast 90 percent of their vote for the Democratic candidate, Jimmy Carter, providing his margin of victory. [10]

Photo by Bernie Noble
The Cleveland Press Collection/Cleveland State University Archives

Carl B. Stokes filing for Mayor, (Cleveland, Ohio)

Although the African-American voter turnout in 1984 was undoubtedly influenced by other factors, such as the steadily increasing registration of African-American voters and resentment of Reagan Administration policies, the Rev. Jesse Jackson's candidacy clearly had a huge impact. The 1984 primaries saw a dramatic increase in African-American voter turnout, with increases of more than 80 percent in some states. In New York, African-American voter participation rose 127 percent.[11] According to the U.S. Census Bureau, African-Americans voted in record numbers in the 1984 Presidential election, up from 48.7 percent in 1976 to 50.5 percent in 1980 to 55.8 percent in 1984. [12]

THE CAMPAIGN OF JESSE JACKSON

Jesse Jackson's 1984 and 1988 Presidential bids marked historic steps in African-American politics. Never before had an African-American been seriously considered as a potential nominee for either the Republican or the Democratic party. As the election of Oscar DePriest in 1928 had done, Jackson's candidacy gave hope to African-Americans that their concerns could be addressed through the electoral process. The 1984 presidential campaign saw the greatest increase in the level and breadth of the African-American participation over any previous campaign.[13] Although initial reaction in the African-American community had been mixed for a number of reasons, Jackson won an average of 66 percent of the African-American vote in the 1984 primary, and 92 percent in the 1988 primary.[14]

During his 1984 campaign, Jackson made the decision to form a "Rainbow Coalition" in order to widen his base of support. The Coalition was an effort to mobilize many groups of disaffected voters into a bloc—not only African-Americans but also other ethnic groups and minorities, women, and the poor.[15] With Jackson's candidacy, African-Americans strongly believed that both they and the Rainbow Coalition could have a significant impact on politics at the national level. Winning only 3.5 million votes in the 1984 primary, Jackson did not obtain the

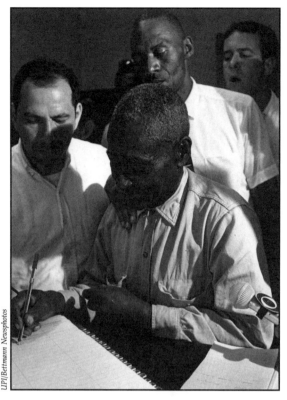

Batesville, Miss.: Registering to vote, 68-year-old Tom Flowers signs his name as he registered at the Panola Co. courthouse here 6/11/66. Flowers registered after the "Mississippi Freedom March" stopped at the courthouse before leaving on 7th day of march to Jackson.

Democratic Party's nomination.[16] But, rather than becoming discouraged and turning away from politics, many African-Americans chose instead to vote in the November election, giving their votes to the Democratic Party, suggesting that they still hoped for a place as full citizens within the traditional two-party system.[17]

In the 1988 primary election, Jackson consciously reached out to voters beyond the Rainbow Coalition, making an anti-drug message a central part of his campaign. He tempered his position on a number of issues to reach a greater range of the electorate, but without "forsaking his role as spokesman for the poor and the powerless."[18] As a result, even lacking the endorsements of a number of prominent black leaders, Jackson was more successful in the 1988 primary election, winning an even greater percentage of the African-American vote and increasing his total primary and caucus vote to 6.6 million; he won 10 primaries or caucuses plus Puerto Rico and the District of Columbia. Furthermore, Jackson's support among white Americans rose to 12 percent, an increase of 7 percent over 1984, and one third of his delegates to the 1988 Democratic National Convention were white.[19]

In 1990, Jackson was elected to the post of "shadow senator" for the District of Columbia. The shadow senator does not actually serve as a senator; rather the shadow senator lobbies the Senate on behalf of a region desiring statehood, in this case, the District of Columbia.

Jesse Jackson's candidacy for the Presidency of the United States in one sense is a measure of the strides African-Americans have made toward achieving full participation in the American political system. However, it also represents the fundamental problem African-Americans still encounter when trying to participate: that of being a significant minority that either must form an independent party or choose whichever of the two parties appears to do the most for them in its platform.[20] Jackson's 1988 campaign slogan was a message of hope—"Keep hope alive" — hope that the disaffected can yet achieve the full equality and recognition guaranteed by the Constitution.

Enormous progress has been made in obtaining the right to vote for African-Americans, but much still remains to be done. Voting is both a challenge and a responsibility. As Roy Wilkins, then director of the NAACP, said in 1964: "Those...who sneer at the ballot box...are overlooking a potent weapon...."[21] The increase in the number of African-Americans who vote has led directly to an increase in the number of African-American elected officials and to greater attention on the part of government, media, and the public to the concerns of African-American citizens. Voting, in the last analysis, is the only way to achieve a government of the people, by the people, and for the people — all people.

CHAPTER **3**

ON THE MOVE: AFRICAN-AMERICAN VOTERS BECOME A POLITICAL FORCE

According to John Hope Franklin, the noted historian, the Reconstruction Era represented "the most dynamic political and economic current that had ever stirred America." [1] African-Americans participated in all the state constitutional conventions held to implement the Reconstruction Act of 1867. (In South Carolina, African-Americans made up the majority of delegates; in Louisiana, the convention membership was divided equally between African-Americans and whites, with 49 delegates each.) African-American participation in these conventions is credited as a key factor in the development of the most progressive state constitutions ever drawn up in the South. The provisions contained in many of these new constitutions abolished property requirements for voting and holding office; some abolished slavery (an action necessary in the states not affected by the Emancipation Proclamation, which only applied to slaves within states in rebellion against the Union), and several sought to eliminate the invoking of race distinctions where the possession or inheritance of property was concerned.

African-American men flocked to the polls in 1870 after the Fifteenth Amendment was passed giving them the right to vote. Whites feared the political power of African-Americans and, as was seen in Chapter I, resorted to violence, intimidation, and legislation to keep African-Americans from exercising their voting rights. The whites who feared losing their dominance in the South had reason to worry, for although the political influence of southern blacks was short-lived, it was powerful while it lasted. African-American voters did play a significant role in reshaping the southern states during Reconstruction, electing a number of African-Americans to local or regional office in the process.

NINETEENTH CENTURY AFRICAN-AMERICAN CONGRESSMEN

Between 1868 and 1896, three African-Americans served in the capacity of lieutenant governor of Louisiana: Oscar J. Dunn, P.B.S. Pinchback, and C.C. Antoine. Indeed, Pinchback actually served as governor for 43 days in the winter of 1873 when elected Governor Henry C. Warmouth was removed from office.

In many southern states, elected African-Americans worked to establish state school systems. In Alabama, African-Americans serving in both houses of the state legislature put a state system of schools into operation as did African-American legislators in North Carolina.

In Florida an African-American, Jonathon Gibbs, served as Superintendent of Public Instruction from 1872 to 1874. While serving in this capacity he organized the state's public school system. Another African-American, H.S. Harmon led the fight for school legislation in Florida.

"We are on the move now. The burning of our churches will not deter us ... We are on the move now. The beating and killing of our clergymen and young people will not divert us. We are on the move now."

African-Americans were also elected to Congress; during the latter half of the nineteenth century, almost as many African-Americans were elected to Congress as have been elected since 1900. Between 1869 and 1901, two blacks served in the U.S. Senate and twenty in the House of Representatives: eight from South Carolina; four from North Carolina; three from Alabama; and one each from Virginia, Georgia, Mississippi, Louisiana, and Florida.

Blanche K. Bruce of Mississippi, elected in 1874, was the only African-American elected to a full term in the U.S. Senate until the election of Edward Brooke

The first seven African-American members of the U.S. Congress during Reconstruction. Senator Hiram Revels and Representatives Benjamin Turner, Robert De Large, Josiah T. Walls, Jefferson Long, Joseph M. Rainey, and R. Brown Elliott.

The Library of Congress

(R) of Massachusetts in 1966. Bruce had been born a slave, but had escaped to Missouri. After the Civil War, he had studied for several years at Oberlin College. Returning to Mississippi, he eventually had amassed a considerable fortune in property and entered politics in 1870. In the Mississippi State Senate he was elected sergeant-at-arms. Later, as a U.S. Senator, Bruce fought for minority rights, investigated election fraud, and proposed a number of bills designed to improve the conditions of African-Americans. After completing his term in the Senate, Bruce was named by President Garfield to the post of Registrar of the U.S. Treasury Department. He held the post until 1885.

Robert C. De Large (South Carolina, 1871-1873) was born a slave in 1842 in Aiken, South Carolina. After receiving what was considered an above-average education, he became a successful farmer during Reconstruction. He served two years in the state legislature before being elected to Congress. The election, however, was marred by serious voting irregularities and a Congressional Commission on Elections declared the seat vacant.

Jefferson F. Long (Georgia, 1869-1871) was born a slave in 1836 near Knoxville, Georgia. Self-educated, he moved to Macon, Georgia at an early age, where he worked as a merchant tailor and eventually opened his own shop. Elected to the 41st Congress, he campaigned vigorously against the spread of lynch laws in Georgia, for the enforcement of the Fifteenth Amendment, and for universal suffrage in the District of Columbia. He died in Macon in 1900.

Hiram R. Revels (Mississippi, 1870-1871) was a free African-American from North Carolina who had lived in Indiana, Ohio, and Illinois. He was educated at a seminary in Ohio and attended Knox College in Illinois. An ordained minister and a school teacher, Revels founded a school for freedmen in St. Louis. After the Civil War, he settled in

Natchez, Mississippi, and was elected to the U.S. Senate in 1870 to fill the seat previously occupied by Jefferson Davis.

Benjamin S. Turner (Alabama, 1871-1873) was born a slave in 1825 in Halifax, North Carolina. He was taken at an early age to Alabama where he was emancipated and given an education. In September of 1870, he was unanimously nominated by the Republican party for the Congressional seat from the 1st District of Selma, Alabama. Although nominated again in 1872, Turner was the victim of a split within his own party, which led to his defeat and eventual abandonment of politics.

Josiah T. Walls (Florida, 1871-1877) was the only African-American Congressman from Florida. He was born free in Winchester, Virginia in 1842. He received his early education in Florida and was a successful farmer by the time the Civil War broke out. After serving one term as a member of the Florida legislature, he was elected in 1871 to the U.S. Congress, where he served during the next five years, until his tenure was interrupted as a result of a contested election and the opposition of the governor. He died in 1905.

Joseph H. Rainey (South Carolina, 1870-1879) was the first African-American member of the U.S. House of Representatives. He was born in Georgetown, South Carolina, in 1832. He escaped to the West Indies and did not return until the Civil War was over in 1865. In 1868 he was elected as a delegate to the state constitutional convention and came to occupy a seat in the state senate. Elected to Congress in 1869, he presented 10 petitions for a civil rights bill that would have guaranteed African-Americans full constitutional rights and equal access to public accommodations. He died in 1887.

R. Brown Elliott (South Carolina, 1871-1875) was born in Boston in 1842 and educated in London, England. He was elected to the South Carolina

constitutional convention and in 1868 won a seat in the lower house of the state legislature. He was elected to the 42nd U.S. Congress and served two terms.

• •

Here are a few of the elected African-American officials who served in the South during Reconstruction:

Francis L. Cardozo	Secretary of State, S. Carolina	1868-72
	Treasurer, S. Carolina	1872-76
Alonzo Ransier	Lieutenant Governor, S. Carolina	1870
Robert Wood	Mayor, Natchez, Mississippi	1870
Richard H. Gleaves	Lieutenant Governor, S. Carolina	1872
Jonathon Gibbs	Superintendent of Public Instruction, Florida	1872-74
Samuel J. Lee	Speaker of the House, S. Carolina	1872
John R. Lynch	Speaker of the House, Mississippi	1872
A. K. Davis	Lieutenant Governor, Mississippi	1873
James Hill	Secretary of State, Mississippi	1873
T. W. Cardozo	Superintendent of Education, Mississippi	1873
Robert Elliott	Speaker of the Assembly, S. Carolina	1874

• •

African-American membership in Congress peaked in the 43rd Congress of 1873-1875 and the 44th Congress of 1875-1877.

AFRICAN-AMERICANS WHO FORMERLY SERVED IN CONGRESS 1869-1991

Jefferson F. Long	Representative	Georgia	1871-1871
Joseph H. Rainey	Representative	South Carolina	1870-1879
Hiram R. Revels	Senator	Mississippi	1870-1873
Robert C. De Large	Representative	South Carolina	1871-1872
Robert B. Elliott	Representative	South Carolina	1871-1874
Benjamin S. Turner	Representative	Alabama	1871-1873
Josiah T. Walls	Representative	Florida	1871-1877
Richard H. Cain	Representative	South Carolina	1873-1875; 1877-1879
John R. Lynch	Representative	Mississippi	1873-1877; 1882-1883
Alonzo J. Ransier	Representative	South Carolina	1873-1875
James T. Rapier	Representative	Alabama	1873-1875
Blanche K. Bruce	Senator	Mississippi	1875-1881
Jeremiah Haralson	Representative	Alabama	1875-1877
John A. Hyman	Representative	North Carolina	1875-1877
Charles E. Nash	Representative	Louisiana	1875-1877
Robert Smalls	Representative	South Carolina	1875-1879; 1882-1887
James E. O'Hara	Representative	North Carolina	1883-1887
Henry Cheatham	Representative	North Carolina	1889-1893
John Mercer Langston	Representative	Virginia	1889-1891
Thomas E. Miller	Representative	South Carolina	1890-1891
George Washington Murray	Representative	South Carolina	1893-1895; 1896-1897
George H. White	Representative	North Carolina	1897-1901
Oscar De Priest	Representative	Illinois	1929-1935
Arthur W. Mitchell	Representative	Illinois	1935-1943
William L. Dawson	Representative	Illinois	1943-1970
Adam Clayton Powell, Jr.	Representative	New York	1945-1971
Charles C. Diggs, Jr.	Representative	Michigan	1955-1980
Robert N. C. Nix, Sr.	Representative	Pennsylvania	1958-1979
Augustus F. Hawkins	Representative	California	1963-1991
Edward W. Brooke, III	Senator	Massachusetts	1967-1979
Shirley Chisholm	Representative	New York	1969-1983
George W. Collins	Representative	Illinois	1969-1972
Ralph Metcalfe	Representative	Illinois	1971-1978
Parren Mitchell	Representative	Maryland	1971-1987
Walter Fauntroy	Delegate	D.C.	1971-1991
Yvonne Brathwaite Burke	Representative	California	1973-1979
Barbara Jordan	Representative	Texas	1973-1979
Andrew Young, Jr.	Representative	Georgia	1973-1977
Bennett Stewart	Representative	Illinois	1979-1981
George T. (Mickey) Leland	Representative	Texas	1979-1989
George W. Crockett, Jr.	Representative	Michigan	1980-1991
Harold Washington	Representative	Illinois	1981-1983
Katie B. Hall	Representative	Indiana	1982-1985
Alton Waldon	Representative	New York	1986-1987

Source: Ragsdale and Treese

AFRICAN-AMERICAN WOMEN— POLITICAL TRAILBLAZERS

African-American women gained the right to vote with other women in 1920 with the passage of the Nineteenth Amendment. African-American women have been politically active in the twentieth century, holding political offices and campaigning for civil rights.

1930s

Mary McLeod Bethune—the only woman to serve in President Roosevelt's "Black Cabinet." She acted as Administrator for the Division of Negro Affairs, National Youth Administration, from 1935 to 1944.

Mary McLeod Bethune, center, looks on as President Truman at his White House desk signs a proclamation designating February first of each year as "National Freedom Day." 7/1/48

1940s

Anna Arnold Hedgeman—The only woman on the administrative committee of the 1963 civil rights march on Washington. From 1944 to 1948 she was the Executive Director of the National Council for the Fair Employment Practices Commission. From 1949 to 1953 she served as an Assistant to the Administrator of the Federal Security Agency (now the Department of Health and Human Services).

1950s

Charlotte Bass—Chosen unanimously by the Progressive Party Convention in 1952 as a vice-presidential candidate. The first African-American woman to run for Vice President.

Carmel Carrington Marr—Former legal advisor to the U.S. mission to the United Nations, appointed in 1953. She was appointed to the Public Service Commission in 1971.

Rosa Parks—Civil Rights Activist. Her actions precipitated the 1955 Montgomery bus boycott, which led to gains in all areas of civil rights.

Edith Sampson—Former alternate delegate to the United Nations. She was the first African-American woman named to the UN, where she served from 1950 to 1953, initially as an appointee of President Harry Truman and later during a portion of the Eisenhower Administration.

1960s

Shirley Chisholm—The first African-American woman to sit in the U.S. House of Representatives. She was elected in 1969 from the 12th District in New York. She announced her candidacy for the Democratic Presidential nomination in 1972.

Shirley Chisholm, the first African-American woman to sit in the U.S. House of Representatives, is flanked by Secret Service agents as she campaigns as a candidate for the Democratic presidential nomination in 1972

35

Zelma George—Appointed as an alternate delegate to the Fifteenth General Assembly of the United Nations in 1960.

Charlotte Moton Hubbard—Appointed in 1964 as Deputy Assistant Secretary of State for Public Affairs, she served in the highest permanent federal position ever held by a African-American woman until her retirement in 1970.

Jewel Lafontant—Former Deputy Solicitor General of the United States. From 1969 to 1983, she was a member of the U.S. Advisory Commission on International, Educational, and Cultural Affairs.

1970s

Mary Frances Berry—Appointed Assistant Secretary of Education by President Carter in 1977, she later became the Commissioner and Vice Chairman of the U.S. Commission on Civil Rights.

Yvonne Brathwaite Burke—The first African-American woman from California to be elected to the U.S. House of Representatives. A former California State Assemblywoman, she was elected to Congress in 1973, representing California's 37th District.

Patricia Roberts Harris—Former Ambassador to Luxembourg, served as Secretary of the Department of Health and Human Services until 1980, and as Secretary of Housing and Urban Development under President Jimmy Carter.

Barbara Jordan—First African-American woman elected to the U.S. House of Representatives from a southern state. She was elected from the 18th district in Texas in 1973.

Sitting in the office of the Speaker of the House at Capitol Hill are six of the 12 Democratic women serving in the 93rd Congress. From (left to right) are Rep. Martha W. Griffiths, Mich.; Rep. Shirley Chisholm, New York; Rep. Elizabeth Holtzman, New York; Rep. Barbara Jordan, Texas; Rep. Yvonne Brathwaite Burke, California; and Rep. Bella Abzug, New York. 1-3-73

Eleanor Holmes Norton—Appointed Chairperson of the Equal Employment Opportunity Commission (EEOC) in 1977. In 1990 she was elected as the District of Columbia delegate to the U.S. House of Representatives.

1980s

Anna Perez—First African-American spokesperson for a first lady (Barbara Bush)

Carrie Saxon Perry—Mayor of Hartford, Connecticut

Dorothy Height—President, National Council of Negro Women

Lenora Fulani—Campaigned as an Independent candidate for President in 1988 (The New Alliance Party). First African-American woman to be on the ballot in all fifty states.

Maxine Waters—Member, California Assembly; member, Democratic National Committee. In 1990, she was elected to the U.S. House of Representatives from California.

1990s

Barbara-Rose Collins—Elected to U.S. House of Representatives from Michigan.

Sharon Pratt-Dixon—Elected mayor of Washington, D.C. in 1990.

Newly elected Democratic Mayor of Washington, D.C. Sharon Pratt Dixon raises her arm in jubilation with campaign manager David Byrd after a landslide victory November 6, 1990

"Let us therefore continue our triumph and march.... Let us march on segregated housing.... Let us march on segregated schools.... Let us march on poverty.... Let us march on ballot boxes."

BENDING TOWARD JUSTICE: SUPREME COURT CASES RELATED TO VOTING RIGHTS

Although the Reconstruction Amendments granted the rights of citizenship and its privileges to African-American men, the scope of these Amendments was repeatedly challenged in the courts. Until the passage of the Voting Rights Act of 1965, case-by-case decisions either extended or denied the right to vote, depending on the Supreme Court's interpretation of the Amendments' scope. Victories in the Supreme Court were costly and slow. The Enforcement Act of 1870 was the first legislative attempt to implement and enforce the Fifteenth Amendment. The act made it a crime to interfere with the right to vote. The following selected cases show how the scope of the Reconstruction Amendments was continually re-interpreted over the years. These decisions shaped the degree to which Constitutional guarantees were afforded to African-American citizens, particularly as they relate to voting.

Minor v. Happerset, 88 U.S. (21 Wall.) 162, 22 L.Ed. 627 (1874)

> *The Court decided that states still had the right to set up their own suffrage, or voting eligibility,*
> *requirements. It took the position that the U.S. Constitution does not confer the right of suffrage upon anyone.*

United States v. Reese, 92 U.S. 214, 23 L.Ed. 563 (1876)

> *Although the Court ruled that the Fifteenth Amendment prohibited certain restrictions on suffrage, it also held that the Amendment conferred no automatic right to suffrage to all.*

Hall v. DeCuir, 95 U.S. 485, 24 L.Ed. 547 (1878)

> *The Court struck down a state Reconstruction law requiring equal accommodations for passengers. Louisiana law required equal rights and privileges for both races on public carriers. A Mississippi River steamboat captain had contested the law by refusing to admit an African-American woman to a "white" cabin because the boat passed through the state of Mississippi. He held that the law interfered with interstate commerce, since integrated cabins were not permitted in every state through which the boat passed.*
>
> *The Court sustained the captain's view and declared the law unconstitutional, ruling in effect that a state could not prohibit segregation on public interstate carriers.*
>
> *The implications for voting rights were evident. Individual states could also segregate public facilities, including polling places.*

Civil Rights Cases, 109 U.S. 3, 3 S.Ct. 18, 27 L.Ed. 835 (1883)

> *The Civil Rights Act of 1875 was the last effort of the Radical Republicans to achieve equality for African-Americans. This act guaranteed equal accommodations in public facilities, such as hotels and theaters, and prohibited racial discrimination in jury selection.*
>
> *Denial of restaurant and inn services in Kansas and Missouri led to two cases. In New York and San Francisco, the denial to African-Americans of the right to attend theaters led to two more cases, and finally, in the former Confederate state of Tennessee, the refusal of a railroad to allow an African-American woman to ride in a ladies railroad car led to the fifth court case.*
>
> *In 1883 all five cases came to the Supreme Court via federal circuit courts. The Supreme Court judges voted eight to one against applicants. One historian has written that "the law was born toothless and stayed that way for nearly a century."* [1]
>
> *In striking down the Civil Rights Act, the Court said that Congress could adopt laws to bar states from denying citizens their rights but could not prevent private individuals or corporations from discriminating.*

Guinn v. United States, 238 U.S. 347, 35 S. Ct. 926, 59 L.Ed. 1340 (1915)

> *The "grandfather clause" was declared null and void.*
>
> *By an amendment passed in 1910, the Constitution of Oklahoma provided that no illiterate person could be registered to vote, but granted an exemption for such a person provided he had lived in a foreign country prior to January 1, 1866, had been eligible to register prior to that date, or if his lineal ancestor was eligible to vote at that time. Since no African-Americans were eligible to vote in Oklahoma prior to 1866, the law disenfranchised all African-American Oklahomans.*

> *The U.S. Supreme Court held that the grandfather clause was invalid in Oklahoma, as well as in any other state where such a provision was in effect.*

Nixon v. Herndon, 273, US 536 (1927)

> *By reason of a state statute providing that no African-American shall be "eligible to participate in a Democratic Party election held in the State of Texas," Dr. L.A. Nixon, an African-American, was denied the right to vote in a Texas primary election. Nixon filed suit against the election officials.*
>
> *In the opinion, the Court said it was beyond argument "that color cannot be made the basis of a statutory classification affecting the rights set up in this case," and therefore declared the Texas statute unconstitutional.*

Nixon v. Condon, 286, US 73 (1932)

> *Following the foregoing decision, the Texas legislature passed a statute empowering the state Democratic executive committee to set up its own rule regarding the primary. The party promptly adopted a resolution stipulating that only white Democrats be allowed to participate in the primary. Dr. Nixon again filed suit, and his right to vote was again upheld by the U.S. Supreme Court.*

Lane v. Wilson, 307 US 268 (1939)

> *In an attempt to restrict voter registration, the Oklahoma legislature had provided that all those who were already registered would remain qualified voters, but that all others would have to register within twelve days (from April 30 to May 11, 1916), or be forever barred from the polls. In 1934 I. W. Lane, an African-American, was refused registration on the basis of this statute. The Court declared that the statute was in conflict with the Fifteenth Amendment of the U.S. Constitution, and as such, was unconstitutional.*

Smith v. Allwright, 321 US 649, 64 S. Ct. 757, 88 L.Ed 987 (1944)

In this case, the Court declared the "white primary" unconstitutional, holding that the Fifteenth Amendment forbade exclusion of African-Americans from primary elections conducted by the Democratic Party.

The Texas State Democratic party, in convention, had limited the right of membership to white electors; non-whites were thus denied the right to participate in the Democratic Party primary. In Grovey v. Townsend (295 US, 45), the Supreme Court had upheld this limitation as not being unconstitutional because determination was made by the party in convention, not by a party executive committee as in Nixon v. Condon (above).

In Smith v. Allwright, the Court overruled Grovey, stating, "The United States is a Constitutional democracy. Its organic law grants to all citizens a right to participate in the choice of elected officials without restriction by any state because of race."

The Court noted that the political party makes its selection of candidates as an agency of the state, and as such, could not exclude participation based on race and remain consistent with the Fifteenth Amendment.

Gomillion v. Lightfoot, 364 U.S. 339, 81 S. Ct. 125, 5 L.Ed. 2d 110 (1960)

In 1957 the Alabama State Legislature passed a law that changed the boundaries of the city of Tuskegee. The change was deliberately designed to exclude African-Americans. Areas where large numbers of African-Americans lived had been gerrymandered so that African-Americans could no longer vote in the city.

The Court found that the law for changing Tuskegee's boundaries was a violation of the equal protection clause of the Fourteenth Amendment.

Baker v. Carr, 369 US 186, 204, 82 S. Ct. 691,703, 7 L.D. 2d 663 (1962)

This landmark case established the "One Man, One Vote" principle.

Baker v. Carr challenged the apportionment of the Tennessee legislature on the grounds that its unequal electoral districts deprived voters of the equal protection of the law guaranteed by the Fourteenth Amendment.

This case was initiated by electors in several counties in Tennessee. The electors asserted that the 1901 legislative reapportionment statute was unconstitutional because the number of voters in the various districts had changed substantially since then.

The plaintiffs requested that the court either direct a reapportionment by mathematical application of the Tennessee constitutional formula to the 1960 census or instruct the state to hold direct at-large elections.

The district court dismissed the case on the grounds that it was a political question and as such, did not fall within the protection of the Fourteenth Amendment.

The U.S. Supreme Court ruled that the case involved a basic constitutional right and thereby was within the court's jurisdiction and remanded the case to the district court.

Reynolds v. Sims 377 US 533, 84 S. Ct. 1362, 12 L.Ed. 2d 506 (1964)

This case is one of several (see Baker v. Carr) referred to as a "One Man-One Vote" case. The Court affirmed the Equal Protection Clauses of the Fourteenth Amendment, which require that the seats in both houses of a bicameral state legislature must be apportioned on the basis of population.

Cleveland Public Library/UPI

In a Charleston, South Carolina primary, Negro voters, for the first time since Reconstruction days, went to the polls on August 11 after Supreme Court decision ruled they could not be deprived of the franchise. 8/11/48

Harper v. Virginia Board of Elections, 383 U.S. 663, 86 S. Ct., 1079, 16 L. Ed 2d 1697 (1966).

This case involved a series of suits filed by Virginia residents demanding that Virginia's poll tax be declared unconstitutional.

The Court concluded that a State violates the Equal Protection Clause of the Fourteenth Amendment whenever it makes the affluence of the voter or the payment of any fee an electoral standard.

Allen v. St. Board of Elections, 393 U.S. 544, 89 S. Ct. 817, 22 LEd. 2d. 1 (1969)

The case was brought by four African-Americans, functionally illiterate voters who were unable to fill out a write-in ballot for a Virginia election. The four had attempted to vote by sticking labels with the names of their chosen candidates in the space provided on the write in ballot. Virginia election officials ruled that their use of labels violated state election laws. The court ruled that the Virginia law constituted "a voting qualification or prerequisite for voting" and thus violated the Voting Rights Act of 1965.

CONCLUSION

As the quotations at the beginning of each section suggest, the march toward African-American suffrage was neither direct nor easy. The quotations, taken from a speech by Dr. Martin Luther King, Jr., following the completion of the Selma-to-Montgomery march, symbolize the historic struggle waged nationwide to obtain the rights of full citizenship—including the right to vote—by African-Americans. One hundred years of detours rooted in tradition and legislation on local, state, and federal levels impeded progress. Yet progress was made, largely because African-Americans believed in the power of the vote.

From Civil War through Reconstruction, despite the Black Codes, violence, literacy tests, the Grandfather Clause, and Jim Crow, not to mention the Supreme Court's changing interpretations of the Fourteenth and Fifteenth Amendments, African-Americans have persisted in their pursuit of the franchise. From the Civil Rights Act to the Voting Rights Act, the journey continues. What lies ahead depends on how African-Americans utilize their political strength and on the continued recognition, especially among younger African-Americans, of the importance of the vote.

"I know you are asking today, 'How long will it take?' I come to say to you this afternoon, however difficult the moment, however frustrating the hour, it will not be long, because truth pressed to earth will rise again.
How long? Not long, because no lie can live forever.
How long? Not long, because you still reap what you sow.
How long? Not long, because the arm of the moral universe . . . bends toward justice."
Martin Luther King, Jr.

AP Wide World Photos Inc

Civil rights marchers. One of the highlights of 1963 was the civil rights march on the capital. The huge crowds which poured into Washington from all over the country jammed the area in front of the Lincoln Memorial and around the Washington Monument Reflection Pool for the civil rights ceremonies. This view was taken from the top of the Lincoln Memorial.

ADDENDA

The road to African-American suffrage did not end in Selma or the courts. The information provided in this section supports the contention that African-Americans have made political gains. It also indicates that much still needs to be done before African-Americans and African-American interests are fully and fairly represented in the United States.

> **AFRICAN-AMERICAN MEMBERS OF THE**
> **102nd CONGRESS OF THE UNITED STATES (1991)**
> All are Representatives. There are no African-American
> Senators in the 102nd Congress.

Year First Elected	Legislator	State (party affiliation)
1968	William L. Clay	Missouri (D)
1973	Cardiss Collins	Illinois (D)
1990	Barbara-Rose Collins	Michigan (D)
1964	John Conyers, Jr.	Michigan (D)
1970	Ronald V. Dellums	California (D)
1978	Julian C. Dixon	California (D)
1980	Mervyn Dymally	California (D)
1986	Mike Espy	Mississippi (D)
1986	Floyd Flake	New York (D)
1974	Harold E. Ford	Tennessee (D)
1990	Gary Franks	Connecticut (R)
1978	William H. Gray III	Pennsylvania (D)
1984	Charles A. Hayes	Illinois (D)
1990	William Jefferson	Louisiana (D)
1986	John Lewis	Georgia (D)
1986	Kweisi Mfume	Maryland (D)
1990	Eleanor Holmes Norton*	District of Columbia (D)
1984	Major Owens	New York (D)
1988	Donald Payne	New Jersey (D)
1970	Charles B. Rangel	New York (D)
1980	Augustus (Gus) Savage	Illinois (D)
1968	Louis Stokes	Ohio (D)
1984	Edolphus Towns	New York (D)
1984	Alan Wheat	Missouri (D)
1989	Craig Washington	Texas (D)
1990	Maxine Waters	California (D)

*Shadow Delegate to Congress representing the District of Columbia

Sources: Ragsdale and Treese and *New Member Orientation*

The Cleveland Press Collection/Cleveland State University Archives

Congressmen William Clay (Missouri), Louis Stokes (Ohio) (pictured), and John Conyers, Jr. (Michigan), elected to Congress in the 1960's, are the senior African-American members of the 102nd Congress.

Table A. Reported Registration, by Region, Race, Hispanic Origin, Sex, and Age: November 1968 to 1988

(Numbers in thousands)

Region, race, Hispanic origin, sex, and age	Presidential elections						Congressional elections			
	1988	1984	1980	1976	1972	1968	1986	1982	1978	1974
UNITED STATES										
Total, voting age	178,098	169,963	157,085	146,548	136,203	116,535	173,890	165,483	151,646	141,299
Percent registered	66.6	68.3	66.9	66.7	72.3	74.3	64.3	64.1	62.6	62.2
White	67.9	69.6	68.4	68.3	73.4	75.4	65.3	65.6	63.8	63.5
Black	64.5	66.3	60.0	58.5	65.5	66.2	64.0	59.1	57.1	54.9
Hispanic origin [1]	35.5	40.1	36.3	37.8	44.4	(NA)	35.9	35.3	32.9	34.9
Male	65.2	67.3	66.6	67.1	73.1	76.0	63.4	63.7	62.6	62.8
Female	67.8	69.3	67.1	66.4	71.6	72.8	65.0	64.4	62.5	61.7
18 to 24 years	48.2	51.3	49.2	51.3	58.9	[3]56.0	42.0	42.4	40.5	41.3
25 to 44 years	63.0	66.6	65.6	65.5	71.3	72.4	61.1	61.5	60.2	59.9
45 to 64 years	75.5	76.6	75.8	75.5	79.7	81.1	74.8	75.6	74.3	73.6
65 years and over	78.4	76.9	74.6	71.4	75.6	75.6	76.9	75.2	72.8	70.2
NORTH AND WEST										
Total, voting age	117,373	112,376	106,524	99,403	93,653	81,594	114,689	110,126	102,894	96,505
Percent registered	67.1	69.0	67.9	67.7	73.9	76.5	64.9	65.2	63.8	63.3
White	68.5	70.5	69.3	69.0	74.9	77.2	66.2	66.7	64.9	64.6
Black	65.9	67.2	60.6	60.9	67.0	71.8	63.1	61.7	58.0	54.2
SOUTH										
Total, voting age	60,725	57,587	50,561	47,145	42,550	34,941	59,201	55,357	48,752	44,794
Percent registered	65.6	66.9	64.8	64.6	68.7	69.2	63.0	61.7	60.1	59.8
White	66.6	67.8	66.2	66.7	69.8	70.8	63.2	63.2	61.2	61.0
Black	63.3	65.6	59.3	56.4	64.0	61.6	64.6	56.9	56.2	55.5

NA Not available

Source: U.S. Bureau of Census

Table B. Reported Voting, by Region, Race, Hispanic Origin, Sex, and Age: November 1964 to 1988

(Numbers in thousands)

Region, race, Hispanic origin, sex, and age	Presidential elections							Congressional elections			
	1988	1984	1980	1976	1972	1968	1964	1986	1982	1978	1974
UNITED STATES											
Total, voting age	178,098	169,963	157,085	146,548	136,203	116,535	110,604	173,890	165,483	151,646	141,299
Percent voted	57.4	59.9	59.2	59.2	63.0	67.8	69.3	46.0	48.5	45.9	44.7
White	59.1	61.4	60.9	60.9	64.5	69.1	70.7	47.0	49.9	47.3	46.3
Black	51.5	55.8	50.5	48.7	52.1	57.6	[2]58.5	43.2	43.0	37.2	33.8
Hispanic origin [1]	28.8	32.6	29.9	31.8	37.5	(NA)	(NA)	24.2	25.3	23.5	22.9
Male	56.4	59.0	59.1	59.6	64.1	69.8	71.9	45.8	48.7	46.6	46.2
Female	58.3	60.8	59.4	58.8	62.0	66.0	67.0	46.1	48.4	45.3	43.4
18 to 24 years	36.2	40.8	39.9	42.2	49.6	[2]50.4	[3]50.9	21.9	24.8	23.5	23.8
25 to 44 years	54.0	58.4	58.7	58.7	62.7	66.6	69.0	41.4	45.4	43.1	42.2
45 to 64 years	67.9	69.8	69.3	68.7	70.8	74.9	75.9	58.7	62.2	58.5	56.9
65 years and over	68.8	67.7	65.1	62.2	63.5	65.8	66.3	60.9	59.9	55.9	51.4
NORTH AND WEST											
Total, voting age	117,373	112,376	106,524	99,403	93,653	81,594	78,174	114,689	110,126	102,894	96,505
Percent voted	58.9	61.6	61.0	61.2	66.4	71.0	74.6	47.5	51.9	48.9	48.8
White	60.4	63.0	62.4	62.6	67.5	71.8	74.7	48.7	53.1	50.0	50.0
Black	55.6	58.9	52.8	52.2	56.7	64.8	[2]72.0	44.2	48.5	41.3	37.9
SOUTH											
Total, voting age	60,725	57,587	50,561	47,145	42,550	34,941	32,429	59,201	55,357	48,752	44,794
Percent voted	54.5	56.8	55.6	54.9	55.4	60.1	56.7	43.0	41.8	39.6	36.0
White	56.4	58.1	57.4	57.1	57.0	61.9	59.5	43.5	42.9	41.1	37.4
Black	48.0	53.2	48.2	45.7	47.8	51.6	[2]44.0	42.5	38.3	33.5	30.0

NA Not available

Source: U.S. Bureau of Census

Table C. Characteristics of the Population Reported Having Registered or Voted: November 1988 and 1984

(Numbers in thousands)

Characteristic	1988			1984		
	Number of Persons	Percent registered	Percent voted	Number of persons	Percent registered	Percent voted
Total, 18 years and over	178,098	66.6	57.4	169,963	68.3	59.9
Race and Hispanic origin:						
White	152,848	67.9	59.1	146,761	69.6	61.4
Black	19,692	64.5	51.5	18,432	66.3	55.8
Hispanic 1	12,893	35.5	28.8	9,471	40.1	32.6
Sex:						
Male	84,531	65.2	56.4	80,327	67.3	59.0
Female	93,568	67.8	58.3	89,636	69.3	60.8
Age:						
18 to 24 years	25,569	48.2	36.2	27,976	51.3	40.8
25 to 44 years	77,863	63.0	54.0	71,023	66.6	58.4
45 to 64 years	45,862	75.5	67.9	44,307	76.6	69.8
65 years and over	28,804	78.4	68.8	26,658	76.9	67.7
Years of school completed:						
Elementary: 0 to 8 years	19,145	47.5	36.7	20,580	53.4	42.9
High school: 1 to 3 years	21,052	52.8	41.3	22,068	54.9	44.4
4 years	70,033	64.6	54.7	67,807	67.3	58.7
College: 1 to 3 years	34,264	73.5	64.5	30,915	75.7	67.5
4 years or more	33,604	83.1	77.6	28,593	83.8	79.1
Family income[2]:						
Under $5,000	5,954	47.6	34.7	7,843	49.8	37.5
$5,000 to $9,999	10,929	52.8	41.3	14,594	56.8	46.2
$10,000 to $14,999	15,682	57.4	47.7	18,131	62.9	53.5
$15,000 to $19,999	25,009	63.2	53.5	15,997	65.5	57.1
$20,000 to $24,999	12,296	67.4	57.8	14,790	68.7	61.1
$25,000 to $34,999	22,995	71.9	64.0	25,322	74.2	67.0
$35,000 to $49,999	24,452	77.9	70.3	20,058	79.8	72.9
$50,000 and over	16,990	81.8	75.6	15,160	82.0	76.0
Income not reported	9,594	61.5	54.2	8,355	62.9	56.9

[1] Persons of Hispanic origin may be of any race.
[2] Restricted to members of families. Income in current dollars.

Source: U.S. Bureau of Census

Table 1. Change in number of black elected officials by category of office, 1970-1989

year	Total BEO's N	Total BEO's % Change	Federal N	Federal % Change	State N	State % Change	Substate Regional N	Substate Regional % Change
1970	1,469	-	10	-	169	-	-	-
1971	1,860	26.6	14	40.0	202	19.5	-	-
1972	2,264	21.7	14	0.0	210	4.0	-	-
1973	2,621	15.8	16	14.3	240	14.3	-	-
1974	2,991	14.1	17	6.3	239	-0.4	-	-
1975	3,503	17.1	18	5.9	281	17.6	-	-
1976	3,979	13.6	18	0.0	281	0.0	30	-
1977	4,311	8.3	17	-5.6	299	6.4	33	10.0
1978	4,503	4.5	17	0.0	299	0.0	26	-21.2
1979	4,607	2.3	17	0.0	313	4.7	25	-3.8
1980	4,912	6.6	17	0.0	323	3.2	25	0.0
1981	5,038	2.6	18	5.9	341	5.6	30	20.0
1982	5,160	2.4	18	0.0	336	-1.5	35	16.7
1983	5,606	8.6	21	16.7	379	12.8	29	-17.1
1984*	5,700	1.7	21	0.0	389	2.6	30	3.4
1985	6,056	6.2	20	-4.8	396	1.8	32	6.7
1986	6,424	6.1	20	0.0	400	1.0	31	-3.2
1987	6,681	4.0	23	15.0	417	4.3	23	-25.8
1988	6,829	2.2	23	0.0	413	-1.0	22	-4.3
1989	7,226	5.8	24	4.2	424	2.7	18	-18.2

*The 1984 figures reflect blacks who took office during the seven-month period between July 1, 1983 and January 30, 1984
Credit: Joint Center for Political and Economic Studies

	County		Municipal		Judicial/Law Enforcement		Education	
	N	% Change	N	% Change	N	% Change	N	% Change
1970	92	-	623	-	213	-	362	-
1971	120	30.4	785	26.0	274	28.6	465	28.5
1972	176	46.7	932	18.7	263	-4.0	669	43.9
1973	211	19.9	1,053	13.0	334	27.0	767	14.6
1974	242	14.7	1,360	29.2	340	1.8	793	3.4
1975	305	26.0	1,573	15.7	387	13.8	939	18.4
1976	355	16.4	1,889	20.1	412	6.5	994	5.9
1977	381	7.3	2,083	10.3	447	8.5	1,051	5.7
1978	410	7.6	2,159	3.6	454	1.6	1,138	8.3
1979	398	-2.9	2,224	3.0	486	7.0	1,144	0.5
1980	451	13.3	2,356	5.9	526	8.2	1,214	6.1
1981	449	-0.4	2,384	1.2	549	4.4	1,267	4.4
1982	465	3.6	2,477	3.9	563	2.6	1,266	-0.1
1983	496	6.7	2,697	10.0	607	7.8	1,377	8.8
1984*	518	4.4	2,735	1.4	636	4.8	1,371	-0.4
1985	611	18.0	2,898	6.0	661	4.0	1,438	4.9
1986	681	11.4	3,112	7.4	676	2.3	1,504	4.6
1987	724	6.3	3,219	3.4	728	7.7	1,547	2.9
1988	742	2.5	3,341	3.8	738	1.4	1,550	0.2
1989	793	6.9	3,595	7.6	760	2.9	1,612	4.0

Table 2: Black elected officials in the United States, January 1989

State	Total	Net Change since January 31, 1988	Federal		State				Substate Regional		County		
			Senators	Representatives	Governors	Administrators	Senators	Representatives	Members, Regional Bodies	Other Regional Officials	Members, County Governing Bodies	Members, Other County Bodies	Other County Officials
Alabama	694	252					5	18			71		15
Alaska	4	0						1					
Arizona	12	-1					1	2					
Arkansas	318	-8					1	5					
California	276	-10		4			2	5	4		8	1	2
Colorado	14	-1					1	3					
Connecticut	63	0				1	3	5					
Delaware	23	1					1	2					
District of Columbia	242	-2		1									
Florida	179	3					2	9			12	2	
Georgia	483	25		1			7	23			98		4
Hawaii	1	0											
Idaho	0	0											
Illinois	444	1		3		1	7	14			38	2	1
Indiana	68	1					2	6			13		
Iowa	9	0					1				1		
Kansas	23	-5					1	3			2		
Kentucky	68	-2					1	1			1		
Louisiana	521	-3					5	15			116	1	
Maine	3	0											
Maryland	118	-2		1			5	22			6		
Massachusetts	38	3					1	5			1		
Michigan	306	-10		2		1	2	14			24		
Minnesota	12	0						1					
Mississippi	646	68		1		1	2	20			67	52	4
Missouri	163	-2		2			3	13			3		
Montana	0	0											
Nebraska	4	0					1						

Municipal					Judicial and Law Enforcement						Education			
Mayors	Members, Municipal Governing Bodies	Members, Municipal Boards	Members, Neighborhood Advisory Commissions	Other Municipal Officals	Judges, State Courts of Last Resort	Judges, Other Courts	Magistrates, Justices of the Peace, Constables	Other Judicial Officials	Police Chiefs, Sheriffs, and Marshalls	Other Law Enforcement Officials	Member, State Education Agencies	Members, University and College Boards	Members, Local School Boards	Other Education Officials
30	398				1	13	41	6	6		2		86	2
	2												1	
	4											1	4	
24	147			17		2	37					1	84	
10	44	5		4	1	79		1	1			16	89	
	3					3		1					3	
2	31	2		2			2						15	
3	11								1				5	
1	10		222										8	
15	96	2		2	1	20			1				15	2
15	225	2		3		18	2	1	1				81	2
													1	
18	152	45		18		23		1				2	119	
1	28		4	2		3							9	
	3							1					3	
1	4	1				2							9	
2	47					2	2	1	1	1			9	
19	169			2		8	42	1	15		1		127	
1	1												1	
8	56		1		1	11		3					4	
	13	6					1						11	
10	80			17	1	52	4				1	14	84	
1	3					4			1				2	
25	282			3	1	1	56	10	6				107	8
16	87			6		10		2	2			2	17	
	1												2	

State	Total	Net Change since January 31, 1988	Federal		State				Substate Regional		County		
			Senators	Representatives	Governors	Administrators	Senators	Representatives	Members, Regional Bodies	Other Regional Officials	Members, County Governing Bodies	Members, Other County Bodies	Other County Officials
Nevada	10	0					1	2			1		
New Hampshire	3	2						3					
New Jersey	199	4		1			2	6			7		1
New Mexico	6	0				1					1		
New York	252	2		4			5	16			13		
North Carolina	449	21					3	12			42	2	1
North Dakota	0	0											
Ohio	216	0		1			2	11			1	1	
Oklahoma	115	3					2	3			2		
Oregon	9	-1					2	1			1		
Pennsylvania	139	2		1			3	15					
Rhode Island	10	0					1	5					
South Carolina	373	21					5	16			64	2	2
South Dakota	3	1											
Tennessee	146	1		1			3	10			47		1
Texas	312	12		1			2	13			16		
Utah	1	0											
Vermont	2	1						2					
Virginia	144	18				1	3	7			36		3
Virgin Islands	35	-1			1	1	9			14			
Washington	20	2					2	1			1		
West Virginia	24	1						1					
Wisconsin	24	1					1	4			3		
Wyoming	2	-1					1						
Total	7,226	397	0	24	1	7	101	315	4	14	696	63	34

Credit: Joint Center for Political and Economic Studies

	Municipal					Judicial and Law Enforcement						Education			
Mayors	Members, Municipal Governing Bodies	Members, Municipal Boards	Members, Neighborhood Advisory Commissions	Other Municipal Officals	Judges, State Courts of Last Resort	Judges, Other Courts	Magistrates, Justices of the Peace, Constables	Other Judicial Officials	Police Chiefs, Sheriffs, and Marshalls	Other Law Enforcement Officials	Member, State Education Agencies	Members, University and College Boards	Members, Local School Boards	Other Education Officials
	2					2						1	1	
10	92							1					79	
	1					2							1	
2	30	5				48	1	1					127	
17	262				1	20		3	4				82	
9	101	3		9		28					1		49	
13	47			21		1			1				25	
	2	1				2								
5	42			3	2	34	13	1					20	
	3												1	
17	131	1				1			5			1	128	
2	1													
2	41					9	6		1				25	
13	126	1				15	23		.1		2	6	93	
						1								
6	73			3		1		8	3		10			
1	5					5							5	
	18			1		2	1	1						
	8					3			1				4	
													1	
299	2882	74	227	113	9	425	231	44	50	1	17	44	1,537	14

Table 3: Black Elected Officials as a Percentage of all Elected Officials, by State, January 1989.

State	Blacks as a percentage of voting-age population	Elected Officials		
		Total	Black	% Black
Alabama	22.0	4,315	694	61.1
Alaska	3.8	1,865	4	*
Arizona	2.4	3,191	12	*
Arkansas	12.0	8,331	318	3.8
California	6.0	19,279	275	1.4
Colorado	4.0	8,035	14	*
Connecticut	4.0	9,929	63	0.6
Delaware	13.8	1,227	23	1.9
District of Columbia	65.9	325	242	74.5
Florida	13.0	5,368	179	3.3
Georgia	31.0	6,556	483	7.4
Hawaii	2.2	160	1	0.6
Idaho	*	4,678	0	*
Illinois	16.0	38,936	444	1.1
Indiana	9.0	11,355	68	0.6
Iowa	1.2	17,043	9	*
Kansas	5.0	16,410	23	*
Kentucky	5.0	7,481	68	0.9
Louisiana	27.0	4,985	521	10.5
Maine	*	7,147	3	*
Maryland	24.0	2,032	118	5.8
Massachusetts	4.0	13,888	38	*
Michigan	13.0	19,292	306	1.6
Minnesota	1.2	19,013	12	*
Mississippi	33.0	4,950	646	13.1
Missouri	10.0	17,115	163	1.0
Montana	*	5,646	0	*
Nebraska	2.7	15,064	4	*
Nevada	4.8	1,174	10	0.9
New Hampshire	*	6,883	3	*
New Jersey	12.0	9,345	199	2.1
New Mexico	1.6	2,096	6	*
New York	13.0	26,343	252	1.0
North Carolina	21.0	5,554	449	8.1
North Dakota	*	15,141	0	*
Ohio	9.0	19,750	216	1.1
Oklahoma	6.0	9,290	115	1.2
Oregon	1.2	8,366	9	*
Pennsylvania	8.0	33,242	139	*
Rhode Island	2.5	1,120	10	0.9
South Carolina	26.0	3,692	373	10.1
South Dakota	*	9,249	3	*
Tennessee	15.0	6,841	146	2.1
Texas	11.0	26,987	312	1.2
Utah	*	2,588	1	*
Vermont	*	8,021	2	*
Virginia	18.0	3,118	144	4.6
Washington	2.4	8,032	20	*
West Virginia	3.1	2,838	24	0.8
Wisconsin	5.0	18,238	24	*
Wyoming	*	2,338	2	*
Total	11.1	503,862	7,191	1.4

Alabama 16.1%

*Less than 0.5 percent.
Note: The 35 BEO's in the Virgin Islands are not included in this table, because the Virgin Islands are not included in the 1987 Census of Governments.
Credit: Joint Center for Political and Economic Studies.

ENDNOTES

PREFACE AND INTRODUCTION
[1] New Federalist Papers reprint, The Plain Dealer, sec. A, 13.

[2] Dr. W. E. B. DuBois Keynote address, 20th Anniversary NAACP Conference Washington: Library of Congress, Moorfield Storey Papers, Manuscript Collection, June 27, 1929; As quoted in Katz 420.

[3] Lockhart, Kamisar, and Choper 852.

[4] Blacks outnumbered whites in South Carolina, Mississippi, and Louisiana. Morison and Commager, 1:730.

[5] Franklin 341.

CHAPTER 1
[1] Hofstadter and Ver Steeg 1:236.

[2] Lincoln's Plan, 1865 - at least 10% of the voters must agree to support the U. S. Constitution. Men who had held high Confederate offices were to be disenfranchised. States were to write new constitutions and elect new leaders.

Johnson's Plan, 1865-66 - Lincoln's 10% plan; however, many more ex-Confederates could hold office if they promised loyalty to the federal government. States must ratify the 13th Amendment and agree not to pay Confederate debts.

Congress's Plan, 1866-67 - Johnson's 10% plan. In addition, states must ratify the 14th Amendment.

Congress's Plan, 1867-77 - All ex-Confederate leaders will be disenfranchised. All states must ratify the 14th Amendment. All states must guarantee voting rights for blacks in their new constitution. States would become military districts without the right to govern themselves.

[3] Foner 198-202.

[4] From Laws of the State of Mississippi, Passed at a Regular Session of the Mississippi Legislature, 1875-1876. Cited in Mississippi Black Code. Linden, Brink, and Huntington, 2:554.

[5] Foner 342.

[6] Katz 340.

[7] Morison and Commager 1:761.

[8] Hofstadter and Hofstadter 3:21.

[9] Between 1889 and 1918, 3224 African-Americans were lynched. Ward 44.

[10] Grant carried all but eight states. The African-American vote of some 450,000 gave Grant his popular margin. Morison and Commager 1:765.

[11] Ward 40.

[12] Wesley 265.

[13] Franklin 339.

[14] Franklin 339.

[15] Booker T. Washington wrote to Louisiana Democrats "that he hoped the law would be so clear that 'no one clothed with state authority will be tempted to perjure and degrade himself by putting one interpretation upon it for the white man and another for the black man '" Franklin 340.

[16] Franklin 340.

[17] Buck and Jones 16.

[18] Durham 44.

[19] Franklin 447.

[20] Ploski and Williams 255.

[21] Ploski and Williams 19.

[22] Congressional Record 5061. 89th Congress, 1st Session.

[23] Hofstadter and Ver Steeg 3:462.

[24] U.S. Statutes at Large. 79:437-446.

[25] Ploski and Williams 361.

CHAPTER 2
[1] Morison and Commager 509.

[2] Quoted in Franklin 525.

[3] Morison and Commager 509.

[4] Lockhart, Kamisar, and Choper, 886.

[5] Ward 57.

[6] Ward 57.

[7] Ward 57.

[8] Robinson A1.

[9] "The Dream" 34.

[10] "The Dream" 34.

[11] Reed 20.

[12] Wissing 7.

[13] Gurin, Hatchett and Jackson 254.

[14] Gurin, Hatchett and Jackson ix.

[15] Reed 70.

[16] Gurin, Hatchett and Jackson ix.

[17] Gurin, Hatchett and Jackson 254.

[18] Kalb and Hertzberg 3.

[19] Gurin, Hatchett and Jackson ix.

[20] Gurin, Hatchett and Jackson 54-56.

[21] As reported in Ward 199.

CHAPTER 3
[1] Franklin 322.

CHAPTER 4
[1] Bailey and Kennedy 2:511.

SOURCES CITED

Bailey, Thomas A. and David M. Kennedy, The American Pageant, Vol. II, p. 511, Lexington, MA, 1991.
Buck, Gladys G. and Josephine Buck Jones. The Black Experience. Missouri: Milliken Publishing Co., 1970.

Congressional Record III pt. 4. 89th Congress, 1st Session. "The Dream Then and Now." Life, special issue, Spring, 1988.

Durham, Joseph T. The Black American Struggle for Equal Rights. Illinois: David C. Cook Publishing Co., 1972.

Foner, Eric. Reconstruction: America's Unfinished Revolution, 1863-1872. New York: Harper & Row, 1988.

Franklin, John Hope. From Slavery to Freedom. 3rd ed. New York: Vintage Books, 1969.

Gurin, Patricia, Shirley Hatchett, and James S. Jackson. Hope and Independence: Blacks' Response to Electoral and Party Politics. New York: Russell Sage Foundation, 1989.

Hofstadter, Richard and Clarence F. Ver Steeg eds. Great Issues in American History. Vol. 1, 2, and 3. New York: Vintage Books, 1958-1969.

Hofstadter, Richard and Beatrice K. Hofstadter eds. Great Issues in American History. Vol. 3. New York: Vintage Books, 1982.

The Joint Center for Political and Economic Studies, 1301 Pennsylvania Avenue N.W., Washington, D.C. 20004

Kalb, Marvin and Hendrik Hertzberg. Candidates '88. Dover, MA: Auburn House Publishing, 1988.

Katz, William Loren. Eyewitness: The Negro in American History. 3rd ed. California: David S. Lake Publishers, 1974.

Library of Congress, Photo Duplication Division, Washington, D.C.

Linden, Glenn M., Dean C. Brink, and Richard H. Huntington. Legacy of Freedom. Illinois: Laidlaw, 1986.

Lockhart, William B., Yale Kamisar, and Jesse H. Choper. The American Constitution. 3rd ed. Minnesota: West Publishing Co., 1970.

Morison, Samuel E., and Henry S. Commager. The Growth of the American Republic. Vol. 1 and 2. New York: Oxford University Press, 1969.

New Federalist Papers, distributed by Public Research Syndicated, July 1987 series, reprint The Plain Dealer.

New Member Orientation. 102d Congress, 1990. Committee on House Administration. Frank Annunzio, Chairman.

Ploski, Harry A., and James Williams eds. The Negro Almanac. 4th ed. New York: John Wiley & Sons, 1983.

Ragsdale, Bruce A. and Joel D. Treese. Black Americans in Congress, 1870-1989. Washington, D.C.: U.S. Government Printing Office, 1990.

Reed, Adolph L. The Jesse Jackson Phenomenon: The Crisis of Purpose in Afro-American Politics. New Haven: Yale University Press, 1986.

Robinson, Mike. "Senate can't override Bush civil rights veto." The Plain Dealer (Cleveland, Ohio), 25 Oct. 1990.

U.S. Bureau of Census, Current Population Reports, Series P-20, #440, Voting and Registration In the Election of November 1988, Washington, D.C.: U.S. Government Printing Office, 1989.

Election of November 1988, Washington, D.C.: U.S. Government Printing Office, 1989.

Ward, Baldwin H., ed. Pictorial History of the Black American. New York: Year, Inc., 1968.

Wesley, Charles H. The Quest for Equality. New York: Publishers Co., Inc., 1968.

Wissing, Beth. Election '84 Wrap-Up. Washington, D.C.: League of Women Voters Education Fund, 1985.

ADDITIONAL RESOURCES

The African-American Museum, 1765 Crawford Road, Cleveland, Ohio 44106.

"The Black Vote." American Visions, February, 1988, Vol. 3, No. 1, pp. 38-40.

"Blacks in Politics: Reconstruction to Present." The (Cleveland, Ohio) Call & Post, 11 February, 1988, pp. 1B-9B.

Carter, Dan T. When the War was Over: The Failure of Self-Reconstruction in the South, 1865-1867. Baton Rouge: Louisiana State University Press, 1985.

DuBois, W. E. B. Black Reconstruction. New York: Harcourt Brace, 1935.

Foner, Eric. Politics and Ideology in the Age of the Civil War. New York: Oxford University Press, 1980.

The National Afro-American Museum and Cultural Center, Wilberforce, Ohio 45384.

Randall, J.G. & David Donald. The Civil War and Reconstruction. 2nd Ed. Boston: Little, Brown, 1969.

Reich, Jerome R., and Edward L. Biller. United States History. New York: Holt, Rinehart and Winston, 1988.

Thernstrom, Abigail M. Whose Votes Count?. Massachusetts: Harvard University Press, 1987.

Woodward, C. Vann. The Strange Career of Jim Crow. New York: Oxford University Press, 1966.